# RITUALS FOR SHARING FAITH

A Resource for
Parish Ministers

*Edited by*
*John Roberto*

THE WORLD OF
## DON BOSCO
### MULTIMEDIA

**NEW ROCHELLE, NY**

*Rituals for Sharing Faith: A Resource for Parish Ministers* is published as part of the Catholic Families Series—resources to promote faith growth in Families. Materials available for parish and diocesan leaders, parents and families

Available titles:

For leaders and ministers:
*Families and Young Adults*
*Families and Youth*
*Families and Young Adolescents*
*Growing in Faith: A Catholic Family Sourcebook*
*Media, Faith, and Families: A Parish Ministry Guide*
*Faith and Families: A Parish Program for Parenting in Faith Growth*

For parents and families:
*Families Nurturing Faith: A Parents' Guide to the Preschool Years*
*Families Sharing Faith: A Parents' Guide to the Grade School Years*
*Families Experiencing Faith: A Parents' Guide to the Young Adolescent Years*
*Families Exploring Faith: A Parents' Guide to the Older Adolescents Years*
*Families Encouraging Faith: A Parents' Guide to the Young Adult Years*
*·Media, Faith, and Families: A Parents' Guide to Family Viewing*
*Family Rituals and Celebrations*

The Catholic Families Series is a publishing project of Don Bosco Multimedia and the Center for Youth Ministry Development

*Rituals for Sharing Faith: A Resource for Parish Ministers*
©1992 Salesian Society, Inc. / Don Bosco Multimedia
475 North Ave., P.O. Box T, New Rochelle, NY 10802
All rights reserved

Library of Congress Cataloging-in-Publication Data
Rituals for Sharing Faith / edited by John Roberto
p. cm. — Catholic Families Series
Includes bibliographical references.
    1. Ritual and Worship. 2. Family Life.
      I. Roberto, John. II. Rituals for Sharing Faith.
ISBN 0-89944-223-4                    $14.95

Design and Typography by Sally Ann Zegarelli, Long Branch, NJ 07740

Printed in the United States of America

3/92     9 8 7 6 5 4 3 2 1

# ABOUT THE AUTHORS

**Thomas Bright** is a staff member of the Center for Youth Ministry Development where he serves as coordinator of justice ministries. He has served as editor for *Access Guides to Youth Ministry: Justice, Poverty: Do It Justice!*, and *Human Rights: Do It Justice!*

**Thomas Boland** is a pastor in the Archdiocese of Louisville, KY and has served as the diocesan director of Family Life Ministry for the Archdiocese of Louisville.

**Angela Erevia, MCDP** a Missionary Catechist of Divine Providence, is diocesan director of Religious Education and Hispanic Ministry for the Diocese of Victoria, TX and the author of *Quince Años: Celebrating a Tradition.*

**Mitch Finley** is a freelance writer, and co-author with his wife, Kathy, of *Christian Families in the Real World: Reflections on a Spirituality for the Domestic Church.*

**Mark R. Francis, CSV** is a member of the Word and Worship faculty of Catholic Theological Union in Chicago and the author of *Liturgy in a Multicultural Community.*

**Maureen Gallagher** is the delegate for Parishes in the Archdiocese of Milwaukee and a popular speaker, writer, and teacher on family ministry and family issues.

**Michael Galvan**, a member of the Ohlone tribe, is a pastor in the Diocese of Oakland and serves as the Director of Clergy Formation for the diocese. He holds a Ph.D. in Christian Spirituality. He has published articles on Native American spirituality and catechesis, one of which is included in *Faith and Culture*.

**Thomas F. Lynch** is pastor in the Diocese of Bridgeport, CT. He has served as the Family Life Specialist for the National Conference of Catholic Bishops and director of the Family Life Office of the Diocese of Bridgeport.

**Eva Marie Lumas, SSS** is a doctoral student in theology at Catholic University of America and has served as a Christian education consultant for Black communities. She lectures widely and writes on Christian education from a Black perspective. Several of her essays appear in *Families Black and Catholic, Catholic and Black*.

**Gelasia Marquez** is the director of Hispanic Family Life Ministry for the Diocese of Brooklyn, NY and holds a doctorate in psychology. She has created a counseling program for Hispanic families in cultural transition.

**Faith Mauro, RSM** is a staff member of the Center for Youth Ministry Development and project coordinator for the Catholic Families Project. She has served as representative for Youth and Young Adult Ministry for the National Conference of Catholic Bishops.

**Jack Miffleton** is an internationally known lecturer on the religious education of children and is a composer of liturgical music. He is the author of *Sunday's Child—A Planning Guide for Liturgies with both Children and Adults*.

**Gertrud Mueller Nelson** is a specialist in liturgy and ritual, and the author of *To Dance with God—Family Ritual and Community Celebration*. Her clip art adorns many parish liturgical and educational bulletins.

**David Ng** is Professor of Christian Education at San Francisco Theological Seminary. Dave has been involved with youth ministry for much of his career, doing many workshops on confirmation, multicultural youth ministry, and leadership development. He has written *Youth in the Community of Disciples, Developing Leaders in Youth Ministry*, and written many articles.

**Arturo Perez** is the author of *Popular Catholicism—A Hispanic Perspective*.

**John Roberto** is director and co-founder of the Center for Youth Ministry Development. He is the managing editor of the *Catholic Families Series*, and has served as editor for *Growing in Faith: A Catholic Family Sourcebook*; and for *Access Guides to Youth Ministry* on *Evangelization, Liturgy and Worship, Justice*, and *Early Adolescent Ministry*.

**Elisa Rodriguez, SC** is a specialist in Hispanic ministry and catechesis. She has served as USCC regional coordinator of Hispanic Ministry. She is currently on assignment for her religious community.

**Wendy M. Wright** is the author of *Sacred Dwelling—A Spirituality of Family Life* and has taught family spirituality at universities and in churches across the country.

# CATHOLIC FAMILIES PROJECT RITUALS FOR SHARING FAITH DESIGN TEAM

This book in the *Catholic Families Series* was designed and piloted by a team of specialists in family-parish ritual who are involved in the Catholic Families Project.

Faith Mauro, RSM—Project Coordinator
Catherine Abeyta—Archdiocese of Santa Fe
Rev. Thomas Boland—Archdiocese of Louisville
Jim Kemna—Diocese of Jefferson City
Rev. Thomas Lynch—Diocese of Bridgeport
Barbara McDonald—Archdiocese of Louisville
Antoinette Purcell, OSB—Archdiocese of Indianapolis
Joan McGinnis Wagner—University of Dayton

# ACKNOWLEDGMENTS

"Finding God in Family Life" by Wendy M. Wright is reprinted courtesy of *Praying* No. 21 (November-December 1987). Used by permission of National Catholic Reporter Publishing Company.

"Family Rites" by Mitch Finley is reprinted courtesy of *Marriage and Family Living* (October 1987). Used by permission of *Marriage and Family Living*.

"Family as Sacrament" by Maureen Gallagher is reprinted from *The Changing Family*, edited by Stanley Saxton, Patricia Voydanoff, and Angela Ann Zukowski,MHSH (1984). Used by permission of Loyola University Press.

"Role of Ritual and Celebration" by Gertrud Mueller Nelson is reprinted from *Liturgy and Spirituality in Context* edited by Eleanor Berstein, CSJ (1990). Used by permission of Liturgical Press.

"Liturgy Begins at Home: Household Sacraments and Childhood Spirituality" by Jack Miffleton is reprinted from *Sunday's Child—A Planning Guide for Liturgies with both Children and Adults* by Jack Miffleton (1989). Used by permission of The Pastoral Press.

"Culture, Faith, and Ritual" by Mark R. Francis, CSV is reprinted from *Liturgy in a Multicultural Community* by Mark R. Francis, CSV (1991). Used by permission of Liturgical Press.

"Toward an Authentic African American Catholic Worship" by the National Conference of Catholic Bishops is reprinted from *Plenty Good Room—The Spirit and Truth of African American Catholic Worship* (1991). Used by permission of the United States Catholic Conference.

"Characteristics of Hispanic Worship" by Arturo Perez is reprinted from *Popular Catholicism—A Hispanic Perspective* by Arturo Perez (1988). Used by permission of The Pastoral Press.

Typist: Alicia Carey

# CONTENTS

# PREFACE TO THE CATHOLIC FAMILY SERIES

"Welcome to the *Catholic Families Series*! In 1987, the Center for Youth Ministry Development began a five-year, three-phase national project, made possible by a generous grant from a Catholic foundation. Guided by the conviction that the family is the primary context for faith growth and faith sharing, the Catholic Families Project was designed to explore the dynamics of faith maturing and faith sharing in Catholic families, and to develop new initiatives for promoting faith maturity in families throughout the entire family life cycle. *Catholic Families: Growing and Sharing Faith* is a unique national effort designed to create new pastoral and educational approaches to fostering faith growth in families. Don Bosco Multimedia is serving as the publisher for these new initiatives by introducing a new line of important resources for *Catholic families* themselves, and for *Church leaders* involved in ministry with families throughout the life cycle.

The Catholic Families Project believes that...

- the family is a community of life and love in service to God's kingdom, with a specific identity and mission
- the family is the primary context for faith growth and faith sharing, profoundly shaping religious identity among its members

- family life is a privileged locale for encountering God in everyday life experiences and in the Christian Tradition/Story
- the family life cycle stages provide a framework for faith growth in the entire family system
- the parish community and its ministries need to be in partnership with the family in nurturing faith growth, in sharing the Catholic Christian faith, and in empowering the family to live the Christian faith both in the family and in the world.

A national effort, the Project has involved over 300 people as authors, critical reflectors, members of design teams and pilot project teams, and as members of the steering committee. These participants represent 70 dioceses and 15 national organizations, as well as the following ministries: higher education; youth ministry; liturgical ministry; lay ministry; rural ministry; special education; ministry with ethnic cultures; and RCIA. This involvement attests to the national and collaborative nature of the Catholic Families Project.

The Catholic Families Project has been conducted along the following timeline:

### 1987—RESEARCH

- Identify how families grow in faith
- Study the patterns and dynamics of sharing faith and values in Catholic Christian families

### 1988—NATIONAL SYMPOSIUM

- Explore and discuss the research base
- Explore and discuss approaches for enriching faith growth and faith sharing in families
- Publish the theoretical-research understandings and pastoral approaches in *Catholic Families: Growing and Sharing Faith*

### 1988–89—PROJECT DEVELOPMENT & PILOTING

- Develop strategies for assisting faith growth throughout the entire family life cycle, incorporating family and cultural perspectives

- Creation and testing of project designs by practitioners in the field

**1991–92—PUBLICATIONS AND CONFERENCES**

- Publish print and audio-visual resources and conduct regional conferences that:
  + offer a family perspective in faith growth and faith sharing
  + address the entire family life cycle
  + forge a partnership between parish and family in promoting faith growth

The Center for Youth Ministry Development and Don Bosco Multimedia are proud to make available the new programs and resources to assist church leaders and families themselves in promoting faith maturing and faith transmission in the family system. These resources fill an important need in the contemporary Church. Included in the *Catholic Families Series* are the following publications:

*Growing in Faith: A Catholic Family Sourcebook*
*Families and Young Adolescents*
*Families and Youth*
*Families and Young Adults*
*Parenting in Faith Growth Series:*
    *Families Nurturing Faith: A Parents' Guide to the Preschool Years*
    *Families Sharing Faith: A Parents' Guide to the School Age Years*
    *Families Experiencing Faith: A Parents' Guide to the Young Adolescent Years*
    *Families Exploring Faith: A Parents' Guide to the Older Adolescent Years*
    *Families Encouraging Faith: A Parents' Guide to the Young Adult Years*
    *Faith and Families: A Parish Program for Parenting in Faith Growth*
*Rituals for Sharing Faith: A Resource for Parish Ministers*
*Family Rituals and Celebrations*
*Media, Faith, and Families: A Parents' Guide to Family Viewing*

*Media, Faith, and Families: A Parish Ministry Guide*
*A Partnership Between Family and Parish: A Pastoral Plan for*
   *the Transmission of Faith*
*Catholic Families Leadership Training Program (Multimedia*
   *Package)*

The importance of developing, supporting, and encouraging the Catholic faith life of families has never been more urgent. The Catholic Families Project is committed to creating and promoting new pastoral and educational approaches for fostering faith growth in families and for building an intentional partnership between families and the parish. *The Catholic Families Series* represents a significant contribution toward realizing these goals.

# INTRODUCTION

The lives of families and parishes are tightly intertwined. Neither can fulfill its task of proclaiming and promoting God's kingdom in the contemporary world without the other. Mutual support and encouragement are essential. Parishes would not exist without the families that people them and provide them with their unique personalities. Families, on the other hand, need the parish community to help them connect with the story of faith and commitment that is broader than their own experience. Ritual celebrations are a key arena in which the lives of the faith community and the family connect.

*Rituals for Sharing Faith: A Resource for Parish Ministers* seeks to make the important connections between the ritual life of the family and the ritual life of the parish community. We are hoping to promote a unique partnership between families and the parish, one that supports and encourages family rituals, while bringing a family perspective to the ritual life of the parish community. *Rituals for Sharing Faith* is designed to help parish leaders build a family perspective in the ritual life of the parish community, to make connections between the ritual life of the parish and the ritual life of the family, and to assist families to identify, utilize, or create, and finally celebrate family rituals. Let us explain.

Rituals are essential for family life. Family rituals give us a sense of permanence, the assurance that even the most ordinary of family activities are meaningful and significant. Many of those who study family life suggest that true meaning in daily living is only accomplished and maintained by family ritual, and that such concrete ways of acknowledging life's meaning are a prerequisite for the physical and emotional health of every family member. The family is able to develop its own sense of permanence and continuity by taking the time to fully attend to the simplest of family activities; by going beyond just "getting things done" to enjoying the sharing of doing things together; by acting with a sense of the honor conferred by the basic activities of family life, which are not chores or obligations, but opportunities to "be" together.

Ritual is born of celebration of family togetherness, through attention to and enjoyment of shared life activities which develop the family bond. Family ritual is making the effort to impart dignity and symbolism to the simple acts of eating together, going to bed, and rising in the morning. Family ritual is attempting to "share" rather than just "do" what life requires. Family ritual is not just saying grace at the dinner table; it is making the effort to help all of the family experience grace together, through the simple act of attending fully to being together for a meal. Whether it is ritualizing everyday patterns like getting up, eating together, or going to bed; or celebrating important milestones, like birthdays and graduations, the family needs to establish rituals which acknowledge life's meaning.

One of the ways that we encounter God is through the experiences and events of everyday life—in our work, in our relationships, and in our family life. Families may not be accustomed to recognizing God's presence in the ordinary events of family life, but each family ritual has the potential of helping families discover God's presence. The rituals of everyday family life and of important milestones are opportunities to share faith in the family. It only takes a little planning and creativity on the part of families to bring faith values into daily life and special occasions. The family's task is to identify and establish their own family rituals so that these rituals may enrich family relationships and help them discover God in their family life.

In addition to the rituals of daily life and important milestones, the Catholic Tradition provides families with a variety of rituals which can provide a sense of permanence to the ways faith is shared in the family. The liturgical year provides families with numerous opportunities for family rituals, especially around Advent and Christmas, Lent and Easter. Civic celebrations, like Martin Luther King, Jr. Day and

Earth Day, likewise provide families with opportunities to celebrate their faith in the family or with other families throughout the year.

Ethnic traditions provide family rituals to celebrate and share the Catholic faith. Ethnic traditions provide a sense of permanence and identity. For some families this will mean affirming the importance of ethnic rituals which have been celebrated in the family for generations. For other families this will mean reclaiming ethnic rituals that have been lost and, perhaps, finding new ways to celebrate these rituals. Ethnic rituals have the power to help families discover and celebrate God's presence.

The parish, likewise, has a ritual life. This ritual life includes the weekly community celebration of Eucharist and regular celebration of Reconciliation and Anointing of the Sick, as well as the ritual milestones of Baptism, Confirmation, and Marriage. The parish ritual life includes celebration of the liturgical year, as well as important church and civic calendar celebrations. In many parishes, ritual life includes celebration of ethnic traditions. The rituals and ceremonials of the parish community significantly shape the faith of its members.

While the process of maturing in faith is complex and diverse, at the heart of faith formation is the family's participation in the Church's rites and sacramental life. John Westerhoff has written, "When we ask, what is most significant in the shaping of *faith...*, *character* (a people's sense of identity and their disposition to behave in particular ways), and *consciousness* (a people's attitudes and awarenesses), the answer is the rituals and ceremonials of a people's primary community. These symbolic actions, words, and behaviors, which express and manifest the community's sacred narrative, significantly influence a people's faith and life." (142) There is tremendous formative influence inherent in ritual ceremonial practices and experiences.

There are definitive moments within the family, the lives of individual family members, and the life of the faith community which offer opportunities for ritual celebration. To uncover the religious significance of life experiences and events families need to recognize and celebrate life cycle events—major rites of passage (like birth, death) *and* rites of growth and transition (like graduations). The faith community needs to assist families in making the connections between the liturgical year celebrations and sacramental celebrations, and the ordinary activities and life cycle events of families. Understanding the stages of the family life cycle provides families and the faith community with numerous opportunities to ritualize and celebrate transitions.

It is our hope that *Rituals for Sharing Faith: A Resource for Parish Ministers* assists you in strengthening the ritual connections between families and the parish community.

## OVERVIEW OF BOOK

**Section 1: Basic Premises** provides an introduction to the key concepts utilized in the Catholic Families Project. These affirmations provide the foundations upon which each resource in the *Catholic Families Series* was developed.

**Section 2: Family and Parish Rituals: Forging a Partnership** contains two essays by pastors of parishes which have been actively working to incorporate a family perspective into parish life and, in particular, into the parish's rituals. These pastoral, practical essays by Thomas Boland and Thomas Lynch make the all-important connections between parish life and family life.

**Section 3: Family and Ritual: Discovering the Possibilities** contains five essays which explore the family life and the potential for ritual celebrations. Each essay provides important insights for discovering the religious significance of family life and for drawing upon the church's ritual life for family celebrations. The essays in this section open up the possibilities for creating a partnership between families and parish.

**Section 4: Family and Ritual: Celebrating Cultural Traditions** provides you with insights on the importance of culture for faith and ritual, as well as specific guidelines for culturally sensitive ministry with families from African-American, Hispanic, Pacific Asian American, and Native American traditions.

**Section 5: Family and Parish Rituals: Making the Connections** by Thomas Bright offers practical suggestions for how parishes can connect with families around the four categories of rituals used in *Family Rituals and Celebrations*—rituals through the year, family milestone rituals, cultural traditions, and rituals through the day. This section includes examples of ritual celebrations and activities for discovering family rituals, created by Faith Mauro, RSM.

# BASIC PREMISES

# ESSAY:
# AFFIRMATIONS FOR FAITH
# GROWTH AND FAITH SHARING
# IN FAMILIES

*JOHN ROBERTO*

The Catholic Families Project has developed a series of affirmations which have guided the development of the five-year project and of the *Catholic Families Series*. These affirmations serve as a conceptual framework around which each book is built and the goals toward which the Catholic Families Project is committed. These affirmations focus on the importance of the family in nurturing and sharing the Catholic Christian faith and in living out this faith in the family and world. They bring a family perspective to the process of faith growth and to the church ministries charged with responsibility for fostering faith growth. Each affirmation is grounded in a broad *understanding* of the role of the family, which is drawn from a variety of sources including developmental research, social science research, family systems theory, theological reflection, and pastoral practice. Each of these affirmations reinforce our belief that it is of the *highest priority* that the family be respectfully understood, critically assessed, and pastorally assisted by the Church today. You will find that *Rituals for Sharing Faith: A Resource for Parish Ministers* utilizes these affirmations in proposing the partnership between families and parish in celebrating rituals.

## AFFIRMATION #1:

THE FAMILY IS A COMMUNITY OF LIFE AND LOVE IN SERVICE TO
GOD'S KINGDOM IN HISTORY WITH A SPECIFIC IDENTITY AND
MISSION. IT HAS THE SAME FUNCTIONS AS THE REST OF THE
CHURCH, BUT IT IS THE CHURCH IN A FAMILY WAY. IT IS *THE
DOMESTIC CHURCH* OR *THE CHURCH OF THE HOME*.

There is a great diversity in definitions of the contemporary
family. In order to focus our work, the Catholic Families
Project utilizes the definition of the family developed by the
United States Catholic Bishops in *A Family Perspective in Church
and Society*:

> ...the family is an intimate community of persons bound
> together by blood, marriage, or adoption, for the whole of
> life. In our Catholic tradition, the family proceeds from
> marriage—an intimate, exclusive, permanent, and faithful
> partnership of husband and wife. The definition is
> intentionally normative and recognizes that the Church's
> normative approach is not shared by all. (19)

While this definition may be restrictive in some senses, it
also proposes a broader view of the family in the following
ways: a) it includes multiple generations and extended family
members; b) it recognizes that many persons are involved
simultaneously in several families; c) it includes single
persons since they have families of origin; d) it recognizes that
there are other covenantal relationships in the family besides
marriage (parent-children, siblings); and e) it recognizes
families that are created by adoption.

Our approach to the contemporary family also recognizes
the great diversity of family structures with nuclear, extended,
single or multiple generations, two-parent, single-parent,
single-earner, dual-earner, childless, blended, and separated
families. We also recognize the diversity in family structures
within particular ethnic groups where family may be viewed
as the entire extended network of relatives or as a wide
informal network of kin and community or as all the ancestors
and their descendents.

The Church teaches that the family has a unique identity and mission that permeates its tasks and responsibilities. This identity and mission is shaped by a Christian vision of family life which views family life as sacred and family activities as holy. The Church sees the family at the service of the building up of the Reign of God. As such the family can be called the *domestic church* or the *church of the home*. The family as a *domestic church* means that the family itself is part of the church. "It has the same functions as the rest of the church, but it is the church in a family way.... Evangelization, catechesis, worship, and ministry will all have their family expressions, but because of the earthly character of family life, they will be rather secular in appearance.... For it is the *life* of the family itself which is its basic spiritual resource. And it is the way in which the love of God and neighbor are joined together in the family that gives it its most fundamental charge" (Thomas 16–17).

## AFFIRMATION #2:

THE MISSION OF THE FAMILY IS TO BECOME AN INTIMATE COMMUNITY OF PERSONS; TO SERVE LIFE IN ITS TRANSMISSION, PHYSICALLY AND SPIRITUALLY; TO PARTICIPATE IN THE DEVELOPMENT OF SOCIETY; AND TO SHARE IN THE LIFE AND MISSION OF THE CHURCH.

## AFFIRMATION #3:

SHARING THE CATHOLIC CHRISTIAN FAITH IN FAMILIES INVOLVES CELEBRATING OUR FAITH THROUGH RITUALS, TELLING THE CATHOLIC FAITH STORY, ENRICHING FAMILY RELATIONSHIPS, PRAYING TOGETHER AS A FAMILY, PERFORMING ACTS OF JUSTICE AND SERVICE, AND RELATING AS A FAMILY TO THE WIDER COMMUNITY.

## AFFIRMATION #4:

WE ENCOUNTER GOD IN THE EXPERIENCES AND EVENTS OF
EVERYDAY LIFE—IN OUR WORK, IN OUR RELATIONSHIPS, IN OUR
FAMILY LIFE—*AND* IN THE CATHOLIC CHRISTIAN STORY—IN THE
SCRIPTURES, IN TRADITION, IN PRAYER, IN THE SACRAMENTS.
FAMILY LIFE IS A PRIVILEGED LOCALE FOR ENCOUNTERING GOD
IN EVERYDAY LIFE EXPERIENCES *AND* IN THE CHRISTIAN STORY.

The mission of the family as a *domestic church*, a community of
life and love in service to God's Kingdom in history, is
realized through four very specific tasks. One of the primary
goals of the Catholic Families Project is to empower families
to undertake and realize these tasks, as well as to assist the
variety of church ministries and their leaders in their work of
empowering families. These four tasks provide the nucleus
around which the *Catholic Families Series* is built. Each resource
seeks to promote the development of these four tasks in the
lives of families. These tasks can be briefly summarized in the
following manner:

**Task 1: The family is an intimate community of persons.**
This community is manifested in mutual self-giving by
the members of the family throughout its life together.
This community also calls for the respect of each family
member's uniqueness and dignity.

**Task 2: The family serves life in its transmission, both
physically by bringing children into the world, and
spiritually by handing on values and traditions as well as
developing the potential of each member at every age.** It
is the duty of parents to create a family atmosphere
inspired by love and devotion to God and their fellow
persons, which will promote an integrated, personal, and
social education of the child. It is the responsibility of all
members of the family to promote the development and
potential of each member at every age.

**Task 3: The family participates in the development of
society by becoming a community of social training,**

hospitality, and political involvement and activity. How family members learn to relate to each other with respect, love, caring, fidelity, honesty, and commitment becomes their way of relating to others in the world.

**Task 4: The family shares in the life and mission of the Church by becoming a believing and evangelizing community, a community in dialogue with God, and a community at the service of humanity.** As the basic community of believers, bound together in love to one another, the family is the arena where the drama of redemption is played out. The dying and rising with Christ is most clearly manifested. Here, the cycle of sin, hurt, reconciliation, and healing is lived out over and over again. In family life is found the *church of the home*: where each day "two or three are gathered" in the Lord's name; where the hungry are fed; where the thirsty are given drink; where the sick are comforted (*Family Perspective* 20, 21, 22).

These four tasks point to specific ways that we can empower families to share the Catholic Christian faith. The Catholic Families Project has identified six specific ways that families share faith and promote the faith growth of family members. These time-honored ways include: 1) celebrating our faith through rituals; 2) telling the Catholic Faith Story; 3) enriching family relationships; 4) praying together as a family; 5) performing acts of justice and service; and 6) relating as a family to the wider community. Each of these six ways contribute to the complex process of promoting growth toward mature faith.

**Celebrating our faith through rituals** happens when the family celebrates the liturgical year, like Advent and Christmas, Lent and Easter; celebrates the civic calendar, like Martin Luther King, Jr. Day and Earth Day; celebrates milestones or rites of passages, like birthdays, anniversaries, graduations, special recognitions; celebrates ethnic traditions which have been passed down through the generations; celebrates the rituals of daily life, like meal prayer, and forgiveness. These celebrations provide the foundations for a family ritual life in which God is discovered and celebrated through the day, week, month, and year. The family's ritual life is complemented by participation in the ritual life of the parish community with its weekly celebration of the Eucharist; regular sacramental celebrations, like Reconciliation and Anointing of the Sick; and liturgical year celebrations.

**Telling or sharing the Catholic Faith Story** happens when parents share stories from the Scriptures with their children, when families discuss the implications and applications of Christian faith for daily living, when a moral dilemma is encountered and the family turns to the resources of the Catholic faith for guidance, when parents discuss the religious questions their children/adolescents ask. The family's sharing is complemented by participation of children, parents, and/or the entire family in the catechetical program of the parish community.

**Enriching family relationships** happens when the family spends both quality and quantity time together; participates in family activities; works at developing healthy communication patterns which cultivate appreciation, respect, and support for each other; negotiates and resolves problems and differences in positive and constructive ways. Enriching family relationships also involves the parents in developing their marriage relationship or a single parent developing intimate, supportive relationships in his or her life.

**Praying together as a family** happens when families incorporate prayer into the daily living through meal and bed times, times of thanksgiving and of crisis; when parents teach basic prayers and pray with their children. The family's prayer life is complemented by participation in the communal prayer life of the parish community, especially through liturgical year celebrations.

**Performing acts of justice and service** happens when the family recognizes the needs of others in our communities and in our world and seeks to respond. Families act through stewardship and care for the earth; through direct service to others, like the homeless and the hungry; through study of social issues; through developing a family lifestyle based on equality, nonviolence, respect for human dignity, respect for the earth. The family's service involvement is strengthened when it is done together with other families in the parish community.

**Relating as a family to the wider community** happens when the families join together in family support groups or family clusters for sharing, activities, and encouragement; when families learn about the broader church and world, especially the cultural heritages of others in the community or the world; when families organize to address common concerns facing families in the community, like quality education and safe neighborhoods.

# AFFIRMATION #5:

A FAMILY SYSTEMS PERSPECTIVE PROVIDES A WAY OF SEEING THE DYNAMICS OF FAMILY LIFE AS OPPORTUNITIES FOR FAITH TO MATURE AND FOR THE CATHOLIC CHRISTIAN STORY TO BE COMMUNICATED.

A family systems perspective is central to the Catholic Families Project and to the resources in the *Catholic Families Series.* A family systems perspective is a new way of viewing family life. It views the family as a living and developing system whose members are essentially interconnected, rather than a collection of individuals. Through relationships, expectations, and responsibilities people connect the very heart of who they are to other people. The family systems model shows how each person in a family plays a part in the whole system. Since all parts are connected and interdependent, the relationships between the parts are more important than the parts themselves. However, in a family individuals also maintain their own identities, rendering the whole system greater than the sum of its parts. Often times there is tension between the need for togetherness as a family and the need for individual autonomy.

Family systems have roles for its individual members, and family rules which govern family living. Roles, rules, and responsibilities give families balance or equilibrium. All families strive for equilibrium or balance. When change or disruption occurs, the family will always try to come to rest and balance, like a mobile. In striving for equilibrium, families tend to resist change. Change in one family member affects all other members and the whole family.

For all these reasons, communication is the lifeblood of the family. Each family develops a style of communication which can assist or inhibit family functioning, e.g., the way the family addresses togetherness and change.

Therefore, when we speak of family as a system we mean the dynamic interplay of relationships within the family as members confront change, maturity, faith growth, and day to day life. It is the emotional push and pull within a family that serves as a catalyst for change and growth, but also provides focal point(s) for struggle and pain. Effective family functioning provides a positive and healthy context for faith maturing.

Utilizing a family systems perspective we can identify the qualities that assist or inhibit the family from meeting the basic needs of nurturance, autonomy, and intimacy. Family strengths enable families to operate effectively as a system meeting the needs of family members and the family as a whole. Supporting, enhancing, and cultivating the sources of strength in family life, rather than focusing on family problems, positively and significantly affects the quality of family life and the health of family members. The research on family strengths can be briefly summarized in the following categories:

> *Commitment*: an investment of time, energy, spirit, and heart; a strong sense of commitment to stay related during times of transition, difficulty, or crisis. Family members are dedicated to promoting each other's welfare and happiness—and they expect the family to endure. They have a sense of shared responsibility for the family.

> *Time Together*: spend both quality and quantity of time together; share leisure time together. The family has a sense of play and humor.

*Appreciation*: appreciate and respect, affirm and support each other.

*Communication*: develop and use skills in communication, negotiating, and resolving problems and differences in a positive and constructive way.

*Religious and Moral Wellness*: possess a solid core of moral and religious beliefs, promoting sharing, love, and compassion for others. The family teaches a sense of right and wrong. They have a strong sense of family in which rituals and traditions abound. They value service to others.

*Coping with Crisis*: internally drawing on the above strengths, developing adaptability; relying on external resources: social network and community organizations. The family admits to and seeks help with problems.

*Understanding, Affirming Parents* and *Close, Caring Families*: parental harmony, effective parent-child communication, a consistent authoritative/democratic parental discipline, and parental nurturing.

*A Personal, Liberating Faith*: emphasis on God's love and acceptance, establishing and maintaining a close relationship to God, and empowering people to reach out and care for others; developed through daily interaction, structured times of worship, and works of justice and service as a family.[1]

The *Catholic Families Series* sees the support and development of these strengths as essential to creating both a positive and healthy context and for promoting faith growth and faith sharing.

# AFFIRMATION #6:

THE FAMILY IS THE PRIMARY CONTEXT FOR FAITH GROWTH AND FAITH SHARING. THE FAMILY, AND PARENTS IN PARTICULAR, ARE

THE KEY VARIABLE IN NURTURING FAITH GROWTH AND IN
SHARING THE CATHOLIC CHRISTIAN STORY/TRADITION WITH
CHILDREN AND YOUTH. SECOND ONLY TO AN INDIVIDUAL'S FREE
RESPONSE TO GOD, THE FAMILY PROFOUNDLY SHAPES CHIL-
DREN'S AND YOUTH'S RELIGIOUS IDENTITY.

At the heart of the Catholic Families Project and the *Catholic
Families Series* is the belief that the first and most primary
community for sharing faith and for promoting faith growth is
the family. This insight permeates all of the resources and
training developed through the Catholic Families Project. This
insight needs to permeate all church ministries. What makes
the family so central is that, sociologically, it is a primary
group, charged with particular tasks that can only be met in a
primary group.

The family, in its diversity of structures, meets four clusters of needs that are essential for being and well-being: 1) to
*belong* and to experience *being irreplaceable*; 2) to experience
*autonomy* and *agency* (belonging); 3) to participate in *shared
meanings* and *rituals*; and 4) to provide for *bodily well-
being*—nurture, wellness, and care. James Fowler observes that
the family is the context in which we participate in the
forming of a first sense of *identity*—who I am, who I can
become, what I am worth or not worth. In the family, we have
our first and most formative experiences of love relationships
and of relationships in which we participate with loyalty and
care. In *The Hurried Child*, David Elkind helps us to see that
one of the important elements of early socialization for
children is learning the *family's covenant system*: what freedoms
will be given children and what responsibilities will be
expected from them, what achievements are expected and
what support can be counted on, what loyalty will be expected
or required from family members, and what commitment will
be given by those who require it. This is a crucially important
part of pre-school socialization. It has to be reworked and
renegotiated as we move through each of the stages of the
personal and family life-cycle (Elkind 120). This is what
makes families so crucially important for the formation of faith
(Fowler).

Research confirms the fact that parents are potentially the greatest influencers of their children's values, religious belief, and behavior. Some of the reasons parents (and the family system) are so important include:

- [Parents have a] closeness to the child (*proximity*) over a long period of time (*longevity*) (Williams).

- The following elements increase the influence of parents (or other significant adults): a) *modeling*: the effect of example has always been understood to be important; b) *agreement*: when parents agree on the importance of religion to them and the messages they convey are consistent, the power of influence increases; c) *congruence*: example is more powerful when parents talk about their actions and when what they say is consistent with what they do (Williams).

- Parents who talk at home about religious activity and motivation are far more likely to have children who have positive attitudes toward religion (Williams).

- The influence of congregations, parents, schools, and peers is best exercised in a *warm, supportive environment*. In spite of the superior power of parents to influence, if the family relationship lacks warmth, support, and acceptance, most children and adolescents will seek those qualities elsewhere (Williams).

- ...we can say that there are four different ways the family of origin affects the religious imagination of one of its offspring: 1) the relationship between the parents of the child...; 2) the relationship of the parents to one another; 3) the religious devotion of both parents, especially if they are very devout; 4) the perception by the child of the parent as religiously influential, which presumably indicates the parent's explicit attempt to teach religion (Greeley 60).

## AFFIRMATION #7:

CHRISTIAN FAITH IS A GIFT OF GOD WHOSE GRACE TOUCHES THE
INNER CORE OF A PERSON AND DISPOSES ONE TOWARD A LIVED
RELATIONSHIP WITH GOD IN JESUS CHRIST.

A holistic and integrated understanding of the Catholic
Christian faith is essential for empowering families to share
faith and to grow in faith. Drawing upon contemporary
theological understandings, we offer this understanding. Faith
as a *gift* invites a free response to share life in relationship
with God who is the very source of life. This response is a
personal encounter with God in Christ which transforms a
person's way of life. As a response of the whole person,
genuine faith involves an affective dimension, the activity of
trusting; a cognitive dimension, the activity of believing; and
the behavioral dimension, an activity of doing.

As an *activity of trusting*, Christian faith is "an invitation to
a relationship of loyalty to and trust in a faithful God who
saves through Jesus Christ by the power of the Spirit"
(Groome 75). This activity of faith also involves trust in and
loyalty to other persons. As an *activity of believing*, Christian
faith is a particular way of interpreting our experience in light
of the Good News and the continuing tradition of the Church
so that it leads to a deeper and expanded understanding of
living as a Catholic Christian. This activity of faith necessarily
involves the gradual development of deep convictions and a
fuller understanding of the doctrinal expression of the Catholic
faith. As an *activity of doing*, Christian faith is an active
response to the mandate of God's Kingdom—to love God by
loving neighbor, especially in the living and pursuit of justice,
peace, equality, and so on. This activity of faith calls us to
transform the world through "a life of loving service on all
levels of human existence—the personal, the interpersonal,
and the social/political" (Groome 76).

Christian faith is covenantal. It is trust and loyalty,
commitment between persons and within groups that is
ratified and deepened by a shared trust in and loyalty to God

in Jesus Christ. Christian faith as *covenantal* is a dynamic pattern of personal trust in and loyalty to:

- God as the source and creator of all value, as disclosed and mediated in Jesus Christ, and through the Church, as inspired by the Holy Spirit. As such Christian faith is *Trinitarian* faith.

- The actual and coming reign of God as the hope and power of the future, and as intending justice and love among humankind. In this sense Christian faith gives us a horizon and vision, a horizon of hope grounded in a trust in the actual, present and coming reign of God.

- God, in Christ, as the Loving, Personal Redeemer and Reconciler calling us to repent and freeing us from the bondage of Sin. Christ frees us from anxiety about death, from the threat of separation from love, and from our hostility and alienation from each other.

- The Church, as Body of Christ, as visible and invisible extension of the ministry and mission of Christ (Fowler 101).

## AFFIRMATION #8:

GROWTH IN CHRISTIAN FAITH IS A GRADUAL, LIFELONG, DEVELOPMENTAL PROCESS INVOLVING THE INDIVIDUAL AND FAMILY SYSTEM IN A CONTINUING JOURNEY TOWARD MATURITY AS A CHRISTIAN.

Christian faith is a journey, a process of conversion, never a point of arrival. Commitment to and growth of mature faith happens over a long period of time. Growth toward maturity in faith involves both a life-transforming relationship to a loving God and a consistent devotion to serving others. While no complete description of faith maturity is possible, we have identified several core dimensions integral to maturing Christian faith.[2] The *Catholic Families Series* seeks to actively promote these core dimensions of mature Christian faith.

- Trusting in God's saving grace and firmly believing in the humanity and divinity of Jesus Christ.

- Experiencing a sense of personal well-being, security, and peace.

- Integrating faith and life—seeing work, family, social relationships, and political choices as part of one's religious life.

- Seeking spiritual growth through Scripture, study, reflection, prayer, and discussion with others.

- Seeking to be part of a Catholic community of believers in which people give witness to their faith, support and nourish one another, serve the needs of each other and the community, and worship together.

- Developing a deeper understanding of the Catholic Christian tradition and its applicability to life in today's complex society.

- Holding life-affirming Gospel values, including respect for human dignity, commitment to uphold human rights, equality (especially racial and gender), stewardship, care and compassion, and a personal sense of responsibility for the welfare of others.

- Advocating for social and global change to bring about greater social justice and peace.

- Serving humanity, consistently and passionately, through acts of love and justice.

The process of maturing in faith is both an individual journey and a family journey. Human development, faith development, and the family life cycle are all intertwined as a person grows toward maturity in faith. While no theory of human development can explain all the factors that contribute to faith maturing, theories do provide windows through which we can gain a better view of what is happening. The work of James Fowler in faith development studies, and of Betty Carter and Monica McGoldrick in family life cycle studies provide useful constructs or frameworks that we are using in the Catholic Families Project and in the *Catholic Families Series*. But, they must be taken as descriptive of the maturing process, rather than as prescriptive or normative. For example, there are ethnic and socio-economic variables which have a direct bearing on human development, yet they are not fully addressed in these theories. Individuals and families have unique features which go beyond the interpretive power of any one theory.

The stages of faith—and their life tasks and transitions—provide opportunities to promote faith growth in the individual and in the entire family system. The *Catholic Families Series* utilizes Fowler's stages of faith development to describe the faith growth at particular stages of the life cycle and to propose strategies for promoting individual and family faith growth and faith sharing.

The family life cycle stages—and their life tasks and transitions—provide opportunities to promote faith growth in the entire family system across generations. The individual life cycle takes place within the family life cycle, which is the primary context of human and faith development. A family life cycle perspective sees the family as a three or four generational system moving through time in a life cycle of distinct stages with particular tasks to accomplish and challenges to face in order to prepare itself and its members for further growth and development. A family life cycle perspective sees the rites of passage that each life cycle change precipitates as creating opportunities for transformation because the family system unlocks or is more open to change at these times. For example, the Church's basic sacraments revolve around many of these life cycle changes. The *Catholic Families Series* utilizes Carter and McGoldrick's conception of the family life cycle stages to describe family growth and to propose strategies for promoting individual and family faith growth and faith sharing.

Two charts at the end of this chapter outlining the stages of development in faith and the stages of the family life cycle will orient you to the two theories used in the *Catholic Families*

*Series.* Both theories have been developed and refined across more than fifteen years of research.

## AFFIRMATION #9:

THE PARISH COMMUNITY AND ITS VARIETY OF MINISTRIES ARE TO BE IN *PARTNERSHIP* WITH THE FAMILY IN NURTURING THE FAITH GROWTH OF FAMILY MEMBERS, IN SHARING THE CATHOLIC CHRISTIAN TRADITION/STORY, AND IN EMPOWERING THE FAMILY TO LIVE THE CHRISTIAN FAITH IN THE FAMILY AND IN THE WORLD. GROWTH IN FAITH THROUGH THE ENTIRE LIFE CYCLE AND THE SHARING/TRANSMISSION OF THE FAITH STORY IS A COMPLEX PROCESS INVOLVING THE FAMILY, THE COMMUNITY OF FAITH, AND THE MULTIPLE MINISTRIES OF THAT COMMUNITY OF FAITH: LITURGY AND WORSHIP, RITUAL LIFE, RELIGIOUS EDUCA-TION/CATECHESIS, AND SERVICE TO THE WORLD.

The Catholic Families Project is calling for an intentional and planned partnership between parishes and families in the process of fostering faith growth throughout the life cycle. This partnership means bringing a family perspective to the parish's life and ministries as these seek to promote faith growth. We have already identified the six specific ways that families share faith and promote the faith growth of family members: 1) celebrating our faith through rituals; 2) telling the Catholic Faith Story; 3) enriching family relationships; 4) praying together as a family; 5) performing acts of justice and service; and 6) relating as a family to the wider community. Each of these six family ways need to be complemented by particular parish ministries which are organized using a family perspective. No one ministry or institution bears the total responsibility for nurturing faith growth. *It is the partnership between family and the parish and its multiple ministries that provide the most effective means for nurturing faith growth.*

The role of the parish community is extremely important for faith maturing. The systems perspective that was used to examine the family can be applied to the parish community as well. Looking at the entire parish system, six aspects of congregational life were identified in a recent study as promoting maturity in faith and stronger congregational and denominational loyalty. They were 1) formal Christian education programs for adults and children/youth; 2) quality of Sunday worship; 3) service to those in need; 4) personally experiencing the care and concern of other members; 5) perceiving the congregation to be warm and friendly; and 6) perceiving the congregation to encourage questions, challenge thinking, and expect learning. The more that each aspect is present in the congregation the greater the maturity of faith and the stronger the loyalty of the individual member. An additional factor for promoting faith growth is high degrees of faith maturity exhibited by the pastor, educators, and parish leaders (Benson et al.).

## CONCLUSION

The importance of developing, supporting, and encouraging the Catholic faith life of families has never been more urgent. The Catholic Families Project is committed to creating new pastoral and educational approaches for fostering faith growth in families and for building an intentional partnership between families and the parish. The *Catholic Families Series* represents a significant contribution toward realizing these goals.

**END NOTES**

[1] This description of family strengths is summarized from Dolores Curran, *Traits of the Healthy Family* (San Francisco: Harper & Row and New York: Ballantine Books, 1983); Nick Stinnett and John DeFrain, *Secrets of Strong Families* (Boston: Little, Brown, and Co., 1985); Merton and Irene Strommen, *Five Cries of Parents* (San Francisco: Harper & Row, 1985).

[2] This description of the core components of mature faith is adapted from Peter Benson, Dorothy Williams, Carolyn Eklin

and David Shuller, *Effective Christian Education: A National Study of Protestant Congregations* (Minneapolis: Search Institute, 1990).

## WORKS CITED

Benson, Peter, Dorothy Williams, Carolyn Eklin and David Shuller. *Effective Christian Education: A National Study of Protestant Congregations.* Minneapolis: Search Institute, 1990.

Benson, Peter, and Carolyn Eklin. *Effective Christian Education: A National Study of Protestant Congregations—A Summary Report on Faith, Loyalty, and Congregational Life.* Minneapolis: Search Institute, 1990.

Carter, Betty and Monica McGoldrick. "The Family Life Cycle." *Growing in Faith: A Catholic Family Sourcebook.* Ed. John Roberto. New Rochelle: Don Bosco Multimedia, 1990.

Elkind, David. *The Hurried Child.* Reading: Addison-Wesley, 1981.

Fowler, James. "Faith Development through the Family Life Cycle." *Growing in Faith: A Catholic Family Sourcebook.* Ed. John Roberto. New Rochelle: Don Bosco Multimedia, 1990.

Greeley, Andrew. *The Religious Imagination.* New York: Sadlier, 1981.

Groome, Thomas. *Christian Religious Education.* San Francisco: Harper & Row, 1981.

Thomas, David. "Home Fires: Theological Reflections." *The Changing Family.* Ed. Stanley Saxton, et al. Chicago: Loyola University Press, 1984.

Williams, Dorothy. "Religion in Adolescence: Dying, Dormant, or Developing," *SOURCE* 5.4 (December 1989).

# 2

# ESSAY:
# STAGES OF FAITH

*JAMES FOWLER*

## Primal Faith

We all start as infants. A lot that is important for our lives of faith occurs *in utero*, and then in the very first months of our lives. We describe the form of faith that begins in infancy as Primal Faith. This first stage is a pre-language disposition, a total emotional orientation of trust off-setting mistrust, which takes form in the mutuality of one's relationships with parents and others. This enables us to overcome or offset the anxiety resulting from separations which occur during infant development. Jean Piaget has helped us understand infant development as a succession of cognitive and emotional separations toward individuation from those who provide initial care. Earliest faith is what enables us to undergo these separations without undue experiences of anxiety or the fear of the loss itself. One can readily see how important the family is in the nurturing and incubation of this first Primal stage of faith.

## Intuitive-Projective Faith

This is a style of faith that emerges in early childhood with the acquisition of language. Here imagination, stimulated by stories, gestures, and symbols, and not yet controlled by logical thinking, combines with perception and feelings to create long-lasting faith images. These images represent both the protective and threatening powers surrounding one's life. If we are able to remember this period of our lives, we have some sense of how important, positively and negatively, it is in the formation of our life-long orientations in faith. When conversion occurs at a later stage in one's life, the images formed in this stage have to be re-worked in some important ways.

## Mythic-Literal Faith

This emerges in the childhood elementary school years and beyond. Here the developing ability to think logically, through concrete operational thinking, helps one to order the world with categories of causality, space, time, and number. This means we can sort out the real from make-believe, the actual from fantasy. We enter into the perspectives of others. We become capable of capturing life and meanings in narrative and stories.

## Synthetic-Conventional Faith

This stage characteristically begins to take form in early adolescence. Here new cognitive abilities make possible mutual, interpersonal perspective-taking. We begin to see ourselves as others see us. We begin to construct the *interiority* of ourselves and others. A new step toward interpersonal intimacy and relationship emerges. A personal and largely unreflective synthesis of beliefs and values evolves to support identity and to unite one in emotional solidarity with others. This is a very important stage of faith, one which can continue well into adulthood and throughout a person's life.

## Individuative-Reflective Faith

With young adulthood or beyond, the stage we call Individuative-Reflective Faith appears. One begins to critically reflect on the beliefs and values formed in previous stages. In this stage, persons begin to rely upon third person perspective-taking. This means constructing a perspective that is neither just that of the self or reliant upon others, but is somehow above them both—a transcendental ego, if you will. The third person perspective brings objectivity and enables us to understand the self and others as part of a social system. Here we begin to see

the internalization of authority, the development of an execu-
tive ego. This stage brings a new quality of responsibility for
the self and for one's choices. It marks the assumption of the
responsibility for making explicit choices of ideology and
lifestyle. These open the way for more critically self-aware
commitments in relationships and in vocation.

## Conjunctive Faith

At mid-life or beyond, frequently, we see the emergence of
Conjunctive Faith. This stage involves the embrace and integration of opposites, or polarities, in one's life. Now what does
this abstract language mean? It means realizing, in mid-life,
that one is both young and old, that young-ness and old-ness
are held together in the same life. It means recognizing that we
are both masculine and feminine, with all of the meanings
those characterizations have. It means coming to terms with
the fact that we are both constructive people and, inadvertent-
ly, destructive people. St. Paul captured this in Romans 7. He
said, "The good I would do I do not do, the evil I would not
do I find myself doing. Who will save me from this body of
death?"

There are religious dimensions to the reintegration of
polarities in our lives. Mary Sharon Reilly, a Cenacle sister
who specializes in spiritual direction for people at mid-life,
titled a paper she has written on her work, "Ministry to
Messiness." This messiness has to do with the holding
together of polarities in midlife existences.

In the Conjunctive stage, symbol and story, metaphor and
myth, both from our own traditions and from others, seem to
be newly appreciated, in what Paul Ricoeur has called a
second or a willed naiveté. Having looked critically at traditions and translated their meanings into conceptual understandings, one experiences a hunger for a deeper relationship
to the reality that symbols mediate. In that deeper relationship,
we learn again to let symbols have the initiative with us. It is
immensely important to let biblical narrative draw us into it
and let it read our lives, reforming and reshaping, rather than

our reading and forming the meanings of the text. This marks a second naiveté as a means of entering into those symbols.

## Universalizing Faith

Beyond paradox and polarities, persons in this stage are grounded in a oneness with the power of being or God. Their visions and commitments seem to free them for a passionate yet detached spending of the self in love, devoted to overcoming division, oppression, and violence, and in effective anticipatory response to an inbreaking commonwealth of love and justice, the reality of an inbreaking Kingdom of God.

# 3

# ESSAY: STAGES OF THE FAMILY LIFE CYCLE

*BETTY CARTER AND MONICA MCGOLDRICK*

The family life cycle comprises the entire emotional system of at least three, and now frequently four, generations. For one thing the three or four different generations must accommodate to life cycle transitions simultaneously. While one generation is moving toward older age, the next is contending with the empty nest, the third with young adulthood, forming careers and intimate peer adult relationships and having children, and the fourth with being inducted into the system. For example, the birth in a new generation corresponds with child-bearing in the parent generation and with grand-parenthood in the eldest generation. If you look at the middle years of childhood, you see a settling down—roughly the period of the thirties for the parents; then you see grandparents planning for retirement. In adolescence, you see parents dealing with mid-life transition—a 40's reevaluation—and you see grandparents dealing with retirement. Then, as that child we've been following comes to the level of being an unattached adult, ready for marriage and courtship, we see parents dealing with issues of middle-adulthood and with renegotiating their marriage relationship. The grandparents, at this point, begin dealing with dependency and late-adulthood.

## The Single Young Adult

In outlining the stages of the family life cycle, we have departed from the traditional sociological depiction of the family life cycle as commencing at courtship or marriage and ending with the death of one spouse. Rather, considering the family to be the operative emotional unit from the cradle to the grave, we see a new family life cycle beginning at the stage of "young adults," whose completion of the primary task of coming to terms with their family of origin most profoundly influences who, when, how, and whether they will marry and how they will carry out all succeeding stages of the family life cycle. Seen in this way, the "young adult" phase is a corner-stone. It is a time to formulate personal life goals and to become a "self" before joining with another to form a new family subsystem. This is the chance for them to sort out emotionally what they will take along from the family of origin, what they will leave behind, and what they will create for themselves. Of great significance is the fact that until the present generation this crucial phase was never considered necessary for women, who had no individual status in families.

**Key Task:** Accepting emotional and financial responsibility for self

**Second-Order Changes:**
   a.   Differentiation of self in relation to family of origin
   b.   Development of intimate peer relationships
   c.   Establishment of self in work and financial independence

## The Joining of Families Through Marriage: The Couple

The changing role of women, the frequent marriage of partners from widely different cultural backgrounds, and the increasing physical distances between family members are placing a much greater burden on couples to define their relationship for themselves than was true in traditional and precedent-bound family structures. Marriage tends to be misunderstood as a joining of two individuals. What it really represents is the changing of two entire systems and an overlapping to develop a third subsystem.

**Key Task:** Commitment to a new system

**Second-Order Changes:**
   a. Formation of a marital system
   b. Realignment of relationships with extended families to include spouse

## Becoming Parents:
## Families with Young Children

The shift to this stage of the family life cycle requires that adults now move up a generation and become caretakers to the younger generation. Parents gain a new sense of themselves as part of a new generational level with specific responsibilities and tasks in relation to the next level of the family. The central struggle of this phase, however, in the modern two-paycheck (and sometimes two-career) marriage is the disposition of child-care responsibilities and household chores when both parents work full-time. In the single parent family the disposition of child-care responsibilities is extremely critical. The shift at this transition for grandparents is to move to a back seat from which they can allow their children to be the central parental authorities and yet form a new type of caring relationship with the grandchildren. For many adults this is a particularly gratifying transition, which allows them to have intimacy without the responsibility that parenting requires.

**Key Task:** Accepting new members into the system

**Second-Order Changes:**
   a. Adjusting marital system to make space for child(ren)
   b. Joining in childrearing, financial, and household tasks
   c. Realignment of relationships with extended family to include parenting and grandparenting roles

## The Transformation of the Family System in Adolescence

Adolescence ushers in a new era because it marks a new definition of the children within the family and of the parents' role in relation to their children. Families with adolescents must establish qualitatively different boundaries than families with younger children, a job made more difficult in our times by the lack of built-in rituals to facilitate this transition. The boundaries must now be permeable. Parents can no longer maintain complete authority. Adolescents can and do open the family to a whole array of new values as they bring friends and new ideals into the family arena. Flexible boundaries that allow adolescents to move in and be dependent at times when they cannot handle things alone, and to move out and experiment with increasing degrees of independence when they are ready, put special strains on all family members in their new status with one another. This is also a time when adolescents begin to establish their own independent relationships with the extended family, and it requires special adjustments between parents and grandparents to allow and foster these new patterns. Families need to make the appropriate transformation of their view of themselves to allow for the increasing independence of the new generation, while maintaining appropriate boundaries and structure to foster continued family development. The central event in the marital relationship at this phase is usually the "midlife crisis" of one or both spouses, with an exploration of personal, career, and marital satisfactions and dissatisfactions. There is usually an intense renegotiation of the marriage.

**Key Task**: Increasing flexibility of family boundaries to include children's independence and grandparents' frailties

**Second-Order Changes:**
a. Shifting of parent-child relationships to permit adolescents to move in and out of the system
b. Refocus on mid-life marital and career issues

    c.  Beginning shift toward joint caring for the older generation

## Families at Midlife:
## Launching Children and Moving On

This phase of the family life cycle is the newest and the longest because of the low birth rate and the long life span of most adults. Parents launch their children almost 20 years before retirement and must then find other life activities. The most significant aspect of this phase is that it is marked by the greatest number of exits and entries of family members. It begins with the launching of grown children and proceeds with the entry of their spouses and children. It is a time when older parents are often becoming ill or dying. This, in conjunction with the difficulties of finding meaningful new life activities during this phase itself, may make it a particularly difficult period. Parents not only must deal with the change in their own status as they make room for the next generation and prepare to move up to grandparental positions, but also with a different type of relationship with their own parents, who may become dependent, giving them (particularly women) considerable caretaking responsibilities. This can also be a liberating time, in that finances may be easier than during the primary years of family responsibilities and there is the potential for moving into new and unexplored areas—travel, hobbies, new careers. This phase necessitates a restructuring of the marital relationship now that parenting responsibilities are no longer required.

    **Key Task**: Accepting a multitude of exits from and entries into the family system

**Second-Order Changes**:
    a.  Renegotiation of marital system as dyad
    b.  Development of adult-to-adult relationships between grown children and their parents
    c.  Realignment of relationships to include in-laws and grandchildren

   d. Dealing with disabilities and death of parents
      (grandparents)

## The Family in Later Life

Among the tasks of families in later life are adjustments to
retirement, which not only may create the obvious vacuum for
the retiring person, but may put a special strain on a marriage
that until then has been balanced in different spheres. Financial insecurity and dependence are also special difficulties,
especially for family members who value managing for
themselves. And, while loss of friends and relatives is a
particular difficulty at this phase, the loss of a spouse is the
most difficult adjustment, with its problems of reorganizing
one's entire life alone after many years as a couple and of
having fewer relationships to help replace the loss. Grand-
parenthood can, however, offer a new lease on life, and
opportunities for special close relationships without the
responsibilities of parenthood.

   **Key Task**: Accepting the shifting of generational roles

   **Second-Order Changes:**
   a. Maintaining own and/or couple functioning and
      interests in face of physiological decline; explora-
      tion of new familial and social role options
   b. Support for a more central role of middle genera-
      tion
   c. Making room in the system for the wisdom of the
      elderly, supporting the older generation without
      overfunctioning for them
   d. Dealing with loss of spouse, siblings, and other
      peers and preparation for own death; life review
      and integration

# DIVORCE AND REMARRIAGE

Divorce in the American family is close to the point at which
it will occur in the majority of families and will thus be

thought of more and more as a normative event. In our experience as clinicians and teachers, we have found it useful to conceptualize divorce as an interruption or dislocation of the traditional family life cycle, which produces the kind of profound disequilibrium that is associated throughout the entire family life cycle with shifts, gains, and losses in family membership. As in other life cycle phases, there are crucial shifts in relationship status and important emotional tasks that must be completed by the members of divorcing families in order for them to proceed developmentally. As in other phases, emotional issues not resolved at this phase will be carried along as hindrances in future relationships.

Therefore, we conceptualize the need for families in which divorce occurs to go through one or two additional phases of the family life cycle in order to restabilize and go forward developmentally again at a more complex level. Of women who divorce, at least 35% do not remarry. These families go through one additional phase and can restabilize permanently as post-divorce families. The other 65% of women who divorce remarry, and these families can be said to require negotiation of two additional phases of the family life cycle before permanent restabilization. (See the essay by Carter and McGoldrick in *Growing in Faith: A Catholic Family Sourcebook* for a description of these additional stages.)

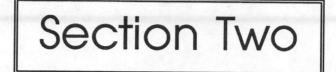

## Section Two

# FAMILY AND PARISH RITUALS: FORGING A PARTNERSHIP

# 1

# ESSAY:
# RITUALS FOR
# LIFE'S PASSAGES

## *THOMAS L. BOLAND*

Like the ceaseless swinging of some giant pendulum, the rhythmic cycle of bonding and separation marks the seasons of our lives. From the moment of our conception till the hour of our death we are plunged into the recurrent challenge of attachment and loss. Bonding in the maternal womb yields to the expulsion of birth. Childhood's delight in family attachments reverses itself in adolescent autonomies. Then in marriage we bond again only to launch our sons and daughters into new independence. And having spent our lives in sealing alliances, we all face the final severance of death's farewells.

For the Christian, life's rhythmic tide of attachment and loss mirrors the Paschal mystery of Christ's dying and rising to new life. Baptized into Jesus' death and his resurrection, the Christian's eyes are opened to the miracle of life born to death, of wealth found in being emptied, and of power proven in vulnerability.

This mystery of new life born of surrender, this Paschal mystery, is proclaimed and preserved in the Church, the Lord's family of the believers. For most believers the Church finds expression in both the parish and in the family. For while the parish church is the context in which the Paschal mystery is authentically proclaimed and celebrated, the church of the home is the arena in which this drama of redemption is played out each day. It is in the family that we are first called and taught to feed the hungry and clothe the naked and comfort the suffering.

The Church uses ritual celebrations to enflesh the mystery of God's saving love and to guide us through life's passages toward our ultimate attachment and fulfillment in God. Rituals in the parish church can often help families understand and embrace the significant times and rites of passage which they inevitably experience. Families who successfully negotiate these critical times grow stronger and more healthy. Families who fail to deal effectively with them face prolonged tension and possible dysfunction.

Effective pastoral ministry with families, therefore, will involve a partnership between the parish church and the home church. Life's most profound passages—through birthing and dying; in bonding and separation—are essentially familial in context. Yet the parish community also has a role: to support, to interpret, and to assist families in these times of passage. Marriage, birth, and death are among the most obvious of life's rites of passage. For centuries the parish church has played a key role in ritualizing them. Through celebrations of weddings, infant baptism, anointings, and funerals the parish community has stood with its families in moments of bonding and of loss. In contemporary society, when families face immense stress and the threat of disintegration due to changing structures, role, and lifestyles, the parish church can still help the home church negotiate life's critical times and passages.

The challenge of parish ministry today is to foster a melding of the formal and universal rituals of the parish church with the intimate and unique experience of each family. Funeral rites, for example, provide a structure and rich resource for assisting bereaved families to face issues of separation, loss, and renewal. But parish leaders must take the time to be with the grieving family, to invite and encourage them to remember together and to tell of the deceased's role in the family story. In a pastoral conference before the funeral, parish leaders and key family members gather for an honest appraisal of hurts and disappointments as well as joys and affections remembered. In the wake service itself there can be a time for remembering and storytelling about the deceased, and in the funeral Mass brief yet focused references can ease the family's grief and give expression to their hope.

In preparing for weddings, more and more parishes are recognizing the value of exploring the family histories of bride and groom, not simply to test for compatibility, but to raise awareness of the unique treasure of experience found in family stories. The wedding ritual itself can facilitate and symbolize the healthy separation which families need to allow in support of the new marital bond which is being forged. Involvement of parents and grandparents in the wedding service can give focus and expression to the new roles and relationships.

Baptism likewise presents opportunities to forge partnerships between the home church and the parish church. The ministry of the parish community is to design preparation programs which foster an awareness of the sacredness of ordinary experience in the Christian family. Through creative and well planned celebrations of the baptismal ritual young parents can come to better understand the important role they play in transmitting the faith from generation to generation.

While the ritual celebrations of life's transitions are specific and precise in the parish church, in the church of the home it is very different. Major life passages are a process, not a moment. Birth follows pregnancy, dying usually is preceded by illness or decline. Coming to maturity is a gradual and ill defined passage without clear beginning or conclusion. In each transition the process of bonding or separation is played out in a procession of small and seemingly insignificant events.

The parish church can assist the church of the home in recognizing and celebrating the significance of these transition times. Occasional blessings at Mass for pregnant mothers, new drivers, college-bound youth, engaged couples, graduates, etc. can remind families and the whole community of the sacredness of those events which occupy so much of their attention at home. Similarly, regular mention of the needs of families, single parents, parents with teens, bereaved families, and the like in petitions of the General Intercessions offers support and encouragement to families.

Some parishes provide special prayer services for families who have lost a child; for those who take care of the elderly; even for the blessing of family pets. Others provide resources for families to use at home on major feasts and holidays. These

simple rituals help families name and celebrate the significance of events that fill their days.

Each parish must fashion its own pattern of partnership
with its home churches according to the diverse needs and
structures of those families. Some partnerships will highlight
ethnic patterns and traditions. Others will seek meaning in
passages shaped by the culture of poverty or of affluence. Still
others will stress the Paschal mystery revealed in brokenness
and family disintegration.

Yet at the heart of any successful partnership is a conviction that the seeds of the sacred are sown for Christian
families in the field of everyday experience. In every age and
from generation to generation they enflesh the Paschal mystery
in their struggle to live the Gospel call to reconciliation,
compassion and love. How fortunate is the parish church
which learns to recognize and celebrate this presence and
power of the Lord in the midst of his people.

# 2

# ESSAY:
# THE RITUAL, PARISH, AND FAMILY CONNECTION

*THOMAS F. LYNCH*

The parish can partner with families in the use of rituals so that the families can celebrate more fully their major rites of passage and their ordinary life experiences. Ritualized celebrations bring the members of a family to a shared experience of the event that they are celebrating. The enhancement of the family's ability to ritualize their lived experience also provides the family with a means to connect with each other at a deeper level. This common experience becomes the glue that binds the story of a family and its members together. They now have a common history rooted in a continuity of future celebrations. In this article, family is understood as a household of faith. A household of faith is established when people have made a commitment of love and faith to one another.

Ritualized celebrations also open to the family and its members a way to enter into the story of a people. The shared actions, words, and symbols of a people connect the family to an experience that is bigger than their own family's experience, such as Thanksgiving or Christmas. This connection can also lead them to connect with God, the source of life itself. This source can give the family the courage and strength needed to continue in their life journey of human love and intimacy.

As the parish community understands the importance of ritualized celebrations for the family in their lived experiences, the parish leadership needs to address how they can be of greater assistance to the family in this regard. This assistance can help families celebrate those somewhat unique but ordinary moments in their lives. The moments of birth, death, covenant love (marriage, religious and public commitment) and the remembering of these moments, as well as the religious celebrations (Advent and Christmas, Lent and Easter) and those ordinary family experiences (praying, grace, going to bed, going off to college, etc.) provide ample opportunities for the parish community to connect with the family. How the parish community connects with the family during these times is the focus of this essay.

The first step for the parish community is to encourage the family to celebrate in fuller ways those unique and ordinary times mentioned above. A consistent reminder to the family can be through bulletin and pulpit announcements. A support group for families, who are willing to encourage each other to be faithful to ritualized celebrations of family events, can be established. These families can commit themselves to engage in the special home prayers and ritual actions for the seasons of Advent/Christmas and Lent/Easter/Pentecost (these special home prayers and ritual actions are contained in this book on family rituals). These families can also celebrate the anniversaries of the death, birth, and covenant love of its members. This group of families can meet twice a year for support. The first meeting is only for the adult members of the household. The second meeting also includes any children that may be in the household. The main objective of the meeting is to encourage, affirm, and share how the families are attempting to celebrate in their own unique way. This also promotes the diversity of family traditions and styles so that families can develop a means of celebration that uniquely reflects who they are.

The goal of this first step is to raise the awareness of the parish community of the necessity of home rituals and the inscribing of as many households in the family support group as possible. This recruitment of the households can come from the many groups (women and senior groups, etc.) and programs (pre-baptism, etc.) that are in the parish. Naming the support group as well as developing a symbol can help in the recruitment.

The second step is more parish-focused. The same prayers and ritual actions that take place in the home during the religious seasons also need to be celebrated in the parish. An example of this is the Advent wreath prayer and lighting, ritualized during daily and Sunday liturgies as well as in the home. As family members hear the prayer and see the action in the parish celebration, it will be a reminder for them to do the same with their family around the home Advent wreath.

During the second stage, the parish blessings given on Father's and Mother's Day, Thanksgiving, Christmas, and Easter are also handed out to family members to be used again in the home. This gives the family the impetus to engage in these blessings at home. They have a sense that they are now part of a larger praying community. They share a common vision of being a Christian household with other families. The critical element in this stage is the common sharing of the blessings between family and parish.

The third step is the consistent teaching of the family that their household of faith is the "church of the home," and that the sacred is revealed in the ordinary events of their shared life. This teaching must permeate all aspects of the life of the parish. The vision of the Church regarding the Christian household needs to be made concrete in the lives of the family. Families need to be called together to reflect on what it means to be a family who is a household of faith: a community of persons; a community committed to the transmission of life; a community participating in the life of society; and a community participating in the life and mission of the Church.

This reflection on the family as a household of faith has to have practical implications for how the family lives and relates to each other and the broader society in which they are members. If this reflection is missing, then the ritualized celebrations of the family can begin to lose its impact. It may also become a ritual practiced without any meaning. These celebrations become a "warm fuzzy" which do not affect how the family members love and relate to each other, the broader society, and the Church. This connection between ritual and reflection becomes extremely important in today's society, which tends to isolate persons and communities.

The fourth step is to bring a family perspective to the major rites of passage. It is important that the family has a better understanding of the dynamic movement that is present in their rite of passage. Consistent education on this topic will assist the family in entering more fully into their rites of passage. The major rites of passage for the family are birth, death, and covenant love (marriage, religious or public commitment). These rites of passage have a process that the family enters: preparatory stage, public act of the event, realignment of familial relationships, and the annual remembrance of the event. For the Christian, the act of remembering becomes the re-experience of the event. In this act of remembrance, the family's positive emotions can be recaptured and the negative ones healed. (The example of marriage in the next essay gives an understanding of the movement that is present in the rite of passage for marriage.)

There are certain attitudes that parish leaders need to have as they seek to incorporate a family perspective in rites of passage. The primary attitude is that the rite of passage belongs to the family. The parish community is only an invited guest who is called to assist the family and its members on their journey. The parish community can provide ministries and rituals along the journey so that the family can more fully enter into what is taking place in their life at a given time. During this time, there is resistance on the part of some family members due to the intensity of emotions that they experience. The letting go and the rejoining in new ways surfaces some of the most ecstatic or painful emotions that reverberate through the life of the family. This may cause greater closeness or confusion and some family disintegration. The parish community can assist the family to remain in the experience and deal with these emotions in ways that are life-giving to the family. Many times on these journeys, the parish community can name and affirm these events as well as give permission for family members to fully open themselves to what is taking place.

The fifth step is for the parish community to create sacred space (shrine or chapel) in which the family and its members can come to pray and to remember major events of their life.

This remembrance can help family members give thanks and/or seek healing and reconciliation. (Remembrance prayers are contained in *Family Rituals and Celebrations*.) By providing the space, the parish community proclaims to the family that they are not alone in their journey. The Christian story with its power of love is with them.

As the parish and family establishes a working partnership, the life of both communities are more fully alive. Their common understanding of the mission of the household of faith becomes a cooperative venture in which the Gospel of love, forgiveness, generosity, and justice is proclaimed. This proclamation also affects the life and vitality of the entire parish community.

# 3

# CASE STUDY:
# THE RITE OF PASSAGE
# OF MARRIAGE: AN EXAMPLE
# OF PARTNERSHIP

## THOMAS F. LYNCH

As pastor of the Parish of St. James in Stratford, CT, I try to facilitate the partnership between the family and our faith community. One of the ways I found to be most effective is the joining of our parish with the family in their rites of passage (birth, marriage, and death). If we, as a community of faith, walk with them during these important moments, the family and its members will have a greater openness to hear the message of the Lord and greater warmth toward our faith community. How the family deals with these rites of passage determines the life and vitality of the family and our community of faith.

The rite of passage of marriage is one example of how the parish community can join with the family and its members as the family celebrates. This rite has five stages: courtship, engagement, the act of marrying, realignment of family relationships, and remembering. Each stage has unique tasks that the family and its members need to accomplish. Even when the family doesn't engage fully in these tasks, the rite of passage still takes place, the major difference being that the experience is not as life-giving for the family. In fact, the passage may cause major disruption and pain, with members of the family even becoming estranged from one another.

The parish community can assist the family at each stage of this rite of passage of marriage through its rituals and ministries so that the family may participate more deeply in these special moments and experience a greater sense of being family.

# COURTSHIP

The first stage is courtship, during which individual members of two families discern whether they can join together the stories and patterns of relationship of both families and form a new reality embracing both families.

The patterns of relationship of the family are established by the way in which each family has dealt with the following: affection, support, decisions, feelings, crises, unity, organization, death/tragedy, faith, communication, expectations, privacy, values, initiative, humor, and rules. During the courtship stage a couple is very much in love. As they begin to understand the depth of the other's family story and patterns, they may realize that the bringing together of these two different family experiences may not work. The couple may become aware that they are unable to accept and deal with the story and patterns of the other family. In fact, they may realize that the wedding of these two family experiences may even produce a destructive pattern within their own relationship, with the potential of destroying their bond of love. This stage brings to the foreground the reality that individuals not only marry each other, but their families as well.

The parish community can assist the family and its members in this stage of courtship by providing opportunities for each family to understand better their generational story and their patterns of relationship. This understanding, and the willingness of each family to hear the story of the other family, helps families decide whether they wish to continue their support of their family member, as he or she decides whether to continue on this rite of passage of marriage.

# ENGAGEMENT

The second stage is called engagement. This is the time when the couple utters a definite "yes" to their willingness to begin the joining together of the stories and patterns of each family into a new reality. They affirm the family of the other as something that they can accept and build upon. They hear anew their childhood stories, those of their beloved, and the feelings surrounding them. They begin to see how unresolved issues in their own childhood and those of their beloved express themselves in symbolic ways in their relationship. They become more aware of the unconscious family-of-origin patterns which are played out in their relationship.

The faith community can assist the family at this engagement stage by celebrating an espousal ceremony, during which a definitive "yes" of the couple can be made by the blessing of the rings of engagement.

The healing of childhood memories and family stories can be now facilitated, and ritualizing the first movement of leave-taking of a member from his/her family of origin can also take place. This is the time to proclaim to the family that its member, whom they have known and to whom they have related, will have to be let go. How they relate to this member is to be changed forever. Also, the member who is leaving must begin the process of letting go of his/her family of origin so that he/she can re-enter their family in a new way.

In the marriage rite, the member becomes "one flesh" with the beloved, and every decision in relationship to his/her family from that moment forth is made in relationship to the beloved.

In this stage of engagement, the family and its members are still free to decide whether they wish to continue this rite of passage of marriage. If they decide in the affirmative, the third stage opens up.

# CELEBRATING THE ACT OF MARRYING

The third stage in the rite of passage for marriage is called the act of marrying. For the Christian, this stage is celebrated in the ritual and story of the Church, bringing greater meaning and depth to the human act of marrying.

This act is now rooted in the proclamation that this couple has been chosen by God to give witness to all people to how our God has loved us unconditionally, faithfully, and forever. This witness is given by how the couple commit themselves to live out their married love and life.

Marriage for this couple is no longer only an act of two families being joined together, but a mission undertaken on behalf of a community of faith. The couple becomes the *church of the home* in which the very presence and power of Jesus Christ is revealed in how they love and forgive one another. Their love, rooted in the love of God, heals the wounds of their childhood and their family stories and patterns. These no longer dominate their relationship. They are freer to establish a new way of being family.

On the wedding day the Church can help make this call to mission visible. Before the couple exchange their vows, they ritually leave their families as their parents pray for, bless, and give an embrace of farewell to them. This leave-taking prepares the couple to enter unconditionally into a permanent covenant with the other. Their mission is now rooted in a new common life. To express this, the couple may be allowed to sit in the chair of the celebrant to symbolize that they are the principal celebrants of the sacrament of marriage and are now called to lead this new union as ministers of the *church of the home.*

After the couple has exchanged their vows, they may lead the married couples who are present in the renewal of their vows. As ministers of the *church of the home*, they may also lead those assembled in the Prayer of the Faithful in which they bless and pray for them.

During the offertory, the couple may bring to the altar a sacrificial gift for those in need symbolizing their commitment to offer a certain percentage of their time, talent, and treasure to others. This proclaims to the assembled community that their home is one of hospitality, not only for their family and friends, but for God's poor.

At the reception, the couple may lead their family and friends in the blessing of food as a gift to those who are gathered with them. During the reception, the families of the bride and groom may ritualize the welcoming of the new family member into their family. This begins the process of the realignment of relationships within both families.

## REALIGNMENT OF FAMILY RELATIONSHIPS

The fourth stage of the rite of passage for marriage is called the realignment of family relationships. For many couples, realignment of family relationships is an opportunity to discover or rediscover the strengths in their families of origin. The opportunity to reflect on the strengths of their families and to build these strengths into their marriage creates a solid foundation for the new family. Realignment also creates the possibilities of reclaiming valued family traditions that may have been put on hold during single young adulthood, but can now be incorporated into the new family. Often times this means rediscovering the power of ethnic traditions and rituals.

For some couples, as their permanent commitment is experienced, the unresolved issues of the family of origin become more intensified and manifest in their relationship. As the couple works through these issues, they each become freer to deal with their family of origin. Unhealthy patterns are faced and changed. A healing and acceptance of past family hurts takes place. As the spouses become freer with their own family of origin and realign those relationships into healthier patterns, they also break some of the unconscious patterns of their spousal relationship. They become freer to see their spouse as he/she truly is and develop a greater capacity to love.

The parish community can be of assistance during this stage of realignment by periodically convening the couple and helping them name their family of origin patterns and strengths, as well as deal with unresolved childhood issues as they surface.

# TIME OF REMEMBERING

The final and ongoing stage of the passage of marriage is the time of remembering. In remembering the sacred moment of their commitment, as well as their efforts of faithfulness to this commitment throughout the years, the couple deepens their original commitment. This remembering brings to the present moment the promises of yesterday with a renewed hope in their tomorrows. The time of remembering also affirms the struggles that they engaged in to love one another in deeper ways. It heals the hurts that have taken place in their relationship.

The parish community can assist the couple in this stage of remembering by creating opportunities for them to come together within the community to remember their day of committed promise. One way that the community can do this is to create a special space in which the couple can come to bless, give thanks, heal, renew, and pray for the other.

At St. James' Parish, we are developing a marriage shrine in our parish center chapel to which couples may come on the day of their anniversary. They are encouraged to give thanks to God for his blessings, and to ask him for his continued blessings. They also engage in a healing ritual that asks the Lord Jesus to intervene in their common life and to heal the hurts that have been sustained over the past year. They are asked to pray for the good of the other and to light a candle in hope for a greater love in their tomorrows.

I believe that if we can enhance the family's rite of passage of marriage by joining with them along their journey, there is a greater witness to all the people of God that committed love is possible in both the human and divine context of life. The above vision is something to which we are committed.

I have learned that the rite of passage of marriage belongs to the family, and that they have most graciously invited our faith community to join with them on their journey. We, the community of St. James, are becoming a more humble, invited guest as we walk with the family in their rite of passage of marriage.

# FAMILY AND RITUAL: DISCOVERING THE POSSIBILITIES

# ESSAY:
# FINDING GOD IN FAMILY LIFE

## *WENDY M. WRIGHT*

A Jesuit friend of mine who has been involved for many years in ministry to Catholic families once reported to me that the response he most often gets to his question, "How does God fit into your lives?" is the hearty affirmation, "Oh Father, we go to church!"

That seems to be the way many believing families—at least in the last several generations—have experienced God most distinctly. God was something or someone you met in a certain place, a church. God was associated with the musky fragrance of incense, the recitation of prayers that had a special, holy language all their own...You met God when you put on your clean, ironed clothes and your clean, ironed behavior and knelt in a heartfelt, if cramped-kneed, gesture of prayer.

If families experienced God within the fabric of their own domestic lives it was in a "churchy" way. Parents and children might gather together before bedtime and recite the Rosary. Or meals were prefaced by solemn prayers. A very Christian home might have its walls decorated with portraits of saints or the pope and celebrate Lenten fasting by forbidding movies or candy. These are indeed ways families have met (and still do meet) God, and there are many healthy Christian lives nourished by such spiritual food.

But I sense today a real distress among many Christian families to whom a God constrained by such a "churchy" identity no longer speaks. This God seems outside the real lives that they live. This God, so clean and ironed, seems unattainable amidst the dirty laundry, the fussing baby, the enormous pressure of a job, and simply making ends meet. This God of respectful silence seems drowned out by the ever-present demands of an active toddler, an exacting employer, a ringing phone. This God seems a stranger to the crucible of intimacy that lives, grows, or dies between a man and a woman. This God is an unbelievable last recourse, not a living presence in a family's anguish with a drug-dependent teen or in the weariness of long years of child-bearing and child-rearing.

My sense is that families today are hungry for a new face of God—not necessarily a new God. (Although some families do make new gods for themselves in money, achievement, or possessions.) There is a continuity, a relationship between the God we find in church and that new face we long to see. What we, as members of Christian families, are looking for is a glimpse of God who we know, deeply within, is truly present to us. Just where we are and what we are. A God who may surprise and greet us in the piles of unwashed laundry as well as in our Sunday best.

All of life is potentially transparent. It can be a window for looking at God. Whatever is around us, as opaque as it might seem, can become a medium through which we glimpse the face we so long to see. By this I do *not* mean that everything, just the way it is, is somehow "willed" by God: that God, like a giant puppeteer, controls the strings of our destinies and prances us around on the stages of our lives so that we must recite our memorized lines and declare that "God plans everything, so everything is just as it should be."

I *do* mean that the vital, dynamic life of our God is present and with us at all times and in all circumstances. It is up to us to look into our lives for signs of that greater and more generous life of which we are a part. There are as many ways of learning to look for these signs as there are people. But I will suggest here three ways that families might go about identifying and experiencing God within the fabric of their daily lives: as presence, as absence, and as presence again.

# PRESENCE

God is present when we are present in one another. We might live in the same house with husband, wife, son, or daughter but we are not always present to one another. We do not often open ourselves to genuinely touch and be touched by our families. And yet family life is an ideal arena in which just such encounters might take place. Every family has both isolated experiences of presence and unique times—I call them "ritual times"—which by their very nature encourage our presence to one another. Here are some examples of such times in which families I know have come to experience each other's and God's presence.

In our own home, bedtime has emerged as the special sacred time of presence for me and my children. It was a time that was forced on me somewhat unwillingly. My first daughter was a very wakeful and irritable infant and could only go to sleep (especially at night) by being soothed and rocked in a darkened room for an extended period of time. For a long time I vacillated between feeling conscientiously maternal and resentful about this ritual. Part of me simply wanted to get quickly into an adult evening and leave the arts of tending behind.

As she grew, my daughter continued to require an extended leave-taking ritual in the form of reading, singing, and comforting touch. As the years unfolded I began to see this time as very special. It became a time in which I was forced to suspend my own agenda, to forget about the next task, to not worry about what was not being accomplished. It became a time in which the two of us could experience, in a heightened way, the mystery of each other's presence. It was a time during which she might offer her reflections on her day or I might pause long enough to really listen. It was a time in which we could enjoy reading together or anticipating events of the next day. It was a time when we blessed one another and exchanged a kiss of peace.

As our other children have come along they have joined our sacred time. Not that we always touch each other and God in this time. The phone does ring, the next day's lunches call out to be packed, there are sometimes guests that need attention, often fatigue or frustration cloud our moment. But then, one evening, we *will* experience each other's presence. We will really listen. We will know ourselves to be moved, to feel how much we love each other. We will see each other with new and gentled eyes.

Another woman I know, a single parent with three teen-aged children, described to me the unusual ritual time that she had discovered in her own family. For many years she could not put the words "family" and "God" together. Her family life was scarred by drug-dependency, verbal and physical abuse, and alcoholism. Often family members would be unable to speak together for days.

Then she recognized their ritual time—a time she realized (once she was encouraged to name it) in which she and her children often discovered presence, each other's and God's. It was at the kitchen sink while washing dishes. She described it as "being inside a bubble." The person washing and the person drying would stand side by side engaged in this household duty and somehow they would begin to talk. They may not have spoken all day. But it was, mysteriously, a shared time in which the unspeakable could be spoken, contact could be made. She reported that no other person ever intruded on this sacred time. Somehow it was tacitly recognized within the family that this ritual moment was set aside, inviolable. A time of presence.

Sexual intimacy between wife and husband also offers the opportunity for the experiencing of presence. Moments of love-making can be moments of profound self-disclosure, times in which the depths of tenderness and communion that we experience in our lives can be expressed. They can be times of emotional and spiritual nakedness, times in which we allow ourselves to be truly touched and changed by another. In genuine unguarded presence, entrusted in the arms of husband or wife, we can experience presence. Present to one another, we are present to God.

Other families I have met have named dinner times—especially holiday dinners—as ritual moments of presence. When those gathered shared food and rehearse, through anecdote, the history of who this family is and where it comes from, presence is experienced.

A young woman student whom I had in a class spoke of walks in the garden with family members as times of presence. Her mother, the hub of their warm, closely knit family, had spent much of her time in the garden. It had been her special place. When her mother died this young woman noticed that the garden became for their family the place where they opened themselves to each other. Often, in groups of two or three, they would walk in their mother's garden and experience a closeness that escaped them anywhere else.

## ABSENCE

It may be a foreign experience for some families to approach God through the medium of presence in their daily lives. It may even be more difficult for families to recognize God in the experience of absence. But God is there. We have a faith that celebrates the fact that God lives and moves intimately within the fabric of human life even in the most desperate and painful of events. We encounter in the experience of absence a different face of our God.

One very simple way families experience God as absence is in their longing for one another when they are apart. Husband and wife may be separated by a job that requires much travel, children may be deprived of a parent by a prolonged illness, or a college-age student may be away at school. In these and other instances, family members miss one another. They long to be reunited, to celebrate presence once again. In the longing itself, a sign of the deep bond of love that connects them, the family can recognize the vibrant touch of God. Love when severed, shattered, or constrained, shows itself as the dark face of absence. Every family knows moments, sometimes long and painful periods, of absence. A quarrel between newlyweds over whose mother to visit on

Thanksgiving, habitual tension between an exacting parent and an unwilling teenager, the desperate loneliness of a couple whose intimate life has turned cold or hostile, the disjointed reality of a family caught in the disease of alcoholism; these are experiences of the absence of God. Yet in the very frustration, even the fearful darkness of our brokenness, God is there. God is there in the very longing we have to be reunited, healed, and whole. God is there in our outrage that this, the family which we look to for nurture, should be so bruised. God is there in the pain of our human limitations and fragility. God breaks and bleeds with us.

I have often thought of the labor of childbirth as being a heightened experience of absence in which the face of God might be discerned. A few women have easy births but the majority of women know something of the pain of bringing children into the world. One may meet the birthing process with a supportive coach; one may even rise to the occasion triumphantly but at some point along the way labor is subjectively an experience of absence. It is at best an experience of exhausting work and at worst a timeless litany of pain. "Why does it have to be so hard?" one woman I know asked. Others accept the challenge of this female rite of passage like triathlon contestants, geared for the rigors of sheer exertions.

My own first childbirth was an encounter with God as absence. A long, unproductive labor unmoored me emotionally. Despite careful preparation and strong resolve, I felt my psychic world crumble away in the onslaught of pain. Later I came to understand how utterly my life was being challenged by the arrival of my first child. This dark passage of absence was in a way expressive of the total reshuffling of my inner and outer world that was to take place through my daughter.

God seemed "withdrawn" because I did not yet recognize any of the new ways God was going to be with me from now on. I was used to meeting God in the restful consolation of prayer, now I would meet a God found in the fatigue of interrupted sleep. I was used to being alone with God, now I would always be accompanied by a small stranger. Even napping, my baby would be with me in my knowledge that she might wake at any time. Yet in the experience of absence

I was being remade, readied to meet God in ways undreamed of, readied to see into the sometimes darkened window of all human life.

## PRESENCE AGAIN

It has been suggested that the primary dynamic of a spirituality of family is forgiveness. I think this is true. Families enter into the very life of God, who is life, in their shared love. They may be more or less open to the fullness of God's life to the extent that they are genuinely present to one another. But most families find it very hard to live out and enflesh their love. We don't communicate well, we anger each other, we are unkind, we are neglectful or openly hurtful.

Yet, as Christians we know we have the mystery of Easter with us. We have the capacity to reclaim our love, to be released from our lack of love by forgiving one another. Genuine forgiveness is not saying a grudging "I'm sorry" or "forget it." It is not tolerating or refusing to confront real abuse. Genuine forgiveness is the ability to see the other as ourselves, to enter into his or her world enough to recognize our shared humanity.

Forgiveness involves knowing that we ourselves fail to love. It is an active participation in the mystery of redemption. In forgiving we do not deny whatever pain has been inflicted nor do we see ourselves as victims deserving of abuse or neglect. Instead, we make a choice to love, to call forth the goodness of husband, wife, or child. We forgive knowing that in the very act of forgiving God is present. Love reclaimed, recalled, remade is an experience of the presence of God again.

It is something of a truism about marriage that real growth in intimacy occurs in the reconciliation after a falling out. That has been my experience. It has not been the times of complacent calm that have brought my husband and I closer together but the time of ruptured love restored. Once, about four years into our relationship, we had a heated argument over some miniscule misunderstanding—the purchase of a gift for a young cousin, I believe. It is hard to remember. But the argument was a memorable one (in part because we do not often erupt at each other). At its most fevered pitch, he stalked out the door. I, enraged at his exit, slammed the door behind him at just the moment he decided to stalk back in. His finger got caught in the door swinging toward him. Shocked by our own vehemence and stunned into recognizing the stupidity of our quarrel, we hurried off to have his finger bound up. About a month later he wrote me a poem, a love poem of forgiveness and praise which ended with the words: "I might still be running, no crack in the door, if that flesh hadn't reached for you, and you, love, caught it."

We discovered a deepened capacity for love, a new humility and expansiveness, in finding God's presence again in the places and people where it has been absent.

Presence, absence, presence again: Our God is with us in joyful moments, in times of pain, in the peace of healing. God wears the faces of those whose lives we share. God is found in our soiled laundry as well as in our Sunday best.

# ESSAY:
# FAMILY RITES—DOIN' WHAT COMES NATURALLY

## *MITCH FINLEY*

Human beings are creatures of symbol and myth. They make sense of their lives by telling stories. They drive away the darkness by lighting candles, saying words, and laying hands on one another.

Many families have never lost the wealth of family rituals. They draw from the wells of their own history and from their religious and cultural roots. Through the years, rituals have been carrying many families through the tragic and comical times of their lives.

But other families have no such resources. Many have lost the ethnic and religious traditions their great-grandparents had taken for granted. In our own culture, unfortunately, many hold dear the fiction that the family can gain vitality through the constant accumulation of material possessions and professional success. This mindset poses an incalculable threat to healthy ways of being family. Until parents face this challenge, there is little sense in talking about family rituals. Once the myths of rampant consumerism are abandoned, however, family-styled religious rituals begin to make sense.

Given parental commitment to a way of life based on an adult understanding of faith, the principle upon which family rituals and family prayer may be based is quite simple. In a family, faith-nourishing rituals must be rooted in the natural events and rhythms of family living.

Parents are sometimes startled to learn of the central spiritual importance of the family's main meal—the evening meal for most families. It has become culturally acceptable to sacrifice family time for outside activities. The school, for example, wants one or more of the kids during the family's dinnertime, and many parents take for granted that the school's demands are a priority. Or an employer asks for overtime. The employer does have that right. Fortunately, many families are beginning to question these demands on their time.

The simple fact of gathering all family members around the table in and of itself is holy. A lighted candle stands in the center of the table, and the family joins hands (or doesn't). Disregarding feelings of embarrassment, they lift their voices in simple song. Traditional and/or spontaneous prayers hover over the mashed potatoes and the cries of a cranky infant or child. The family meal may be the scene of chaos, but it can be easily ritualized all the same. This is good; this is sacred; this is holy.

Adolescent offspring are going to be out till various hours tonight. Before the dash in all directions—maybe right after dinner—the family together, with arms around one another, quietly prays the Our Father.

Parents are sometimes reluctant to start family rituals for fear that whatever they try will seem contrived or unnatural. Parents often discover, however, that soon the family becomes comfortable with a new ritual.

When the children are quite young, bedtime prayers, bedtime blessings, or both are indispensable. Mom or Dad places a hand on the child's head and says, "God be with you all through the night," or whatever words seem best. They can trace the sign of the cross on the child's forehead.

A father who wins no prizes for his singing voice croons to his kids at bedtime: "Swing low, sweet chariot, comin' for to carry me home..." A mother sings, "Puff, the magic dragon, lived by the sea..." Other parents are fond of an old Lime-lighters song:

"Train whistle blowin'
Makes a sleepy noise
Underneath their blankets
Go all the girls and boys..."

A poll of parents would prove the list endless, and every song on the list becomes sacred when used as a celebration to close another day of living.

Birthdays, unfortunately, have become one of our most secularized events. Actually this is a family occasion which carries tremendous echoes of the sacred. Some families resist the temptation to celebrate a child's birthday in a fast-food restaurant. Instead, they recall the unmatchable gift the birthday person is and blend prayers with birthday candles.

Some families make birthdays a week-long affair. Days before a family member's birthday, they have photo albums lying around with pictures of the birthday person to remind everyone of significant times in that person's life. Or while eating birthday cake, they watch a slide show centered on the birthday person. One family gathers outside the family member's bedroom door the morning of his or her birthday and sings "Happy Birthday" as a wake-up song. Then the family attends Mass together that morning in their parish church.

Parents can cultivate a sensitivity, a kind of built-in radar for unique events that will, if tapped, become revelations of the holy. A few years ago, our family gained a new horsey-on-wheels for the three-year-old, a new tricycle for the four-year-old, and a new bicycle for the six-year-old. They were quickly lined up for the official family blessing. We lit a hastily located candle and let each kid hold it while one parent said a quick prayer, asking God to bless the "new wheels" and keep the riders safe.

Some parents have located religious images, that also qualify as good art, to place on the kids' bedroom walls. They walk in procession to music and make the rounds of the kids' bedrooms. They light the candle, hand the icon or picture, say a prayer, sing a familiar song, and chime "Amen."

It's not too late to celebrate the beginning of a new school year. Ignoring the TV, gather pencils, papers, and books together on a table. Light a candle, say a prayer, and sing a song.

Parents hear endlessly that they are the primary religious educators of their children. This has little to do with books, memorizing the Commandments, or learning rules and regulations. Wise parents leave that to the second or third most important form of religious education, the kind that happens in a religious education program. Kids get the most effective religious formation in the family context, and most of it originates in situations that fire the young imagination, evoke wonder, some laughter, and a question or two.

The 16-year-old just received her driver's license. What parent needs to be convinced of the need for prayer at this time? Most parents keep this to themselves—but others don't. Around the dinner table, the family says a prayer for the driver and after the meal, they go out and bless the car.

Opportunities for family rituals are endless. Families ritualize forgiveness and reconciliation with soft drinks or a game of Trivial Pursuit. Family popcorn rituals serve many purposes—spiritual to their roots, because they nourish the bonds of family love.

One of the most important family rituals is the pleasures of the marriage bed. The sexual rituals of marriage sacramentalize the love upon which the family is founded. As this love goes, so goes the family. It is a central family ritual to attend to this rite, to nourish this pleasure—and every married couple knows it isn't always easy.

Making love is a private ritual, of course, which has profound effects on virtually every dimension of a family's life. Husband and wife ritualize their love and witness to God's presence in their relationship in a more public way, however, when they express affection for each other in the presence of their children.

Inevitably, there is the problem of older children who are "too cool" to participate in family rituals. Wise parents should be patient, invite but not coerce, and accept whatever level of participation or nonparticipation the youngster is comfortable with. If the older child decides to join in, it's important that there be a sense of this being "our thing" as a family, not just another peculiar parental idea. Only patience and acceptance from parents allow kids to gradually take this kind of "ownership" in a family ritual.

There is a vital relationship between family rituals and the quality of life in the local parish. Rituals are one of the most important ways to nourish the faith life of family members. Parishes constituted of families and other households where domestic rituals thrive are true communities of faith, places where people like to be. Parish ministers do well to ask themselves what they have done lately to inspire and support religious life in the home. Families need parish ministers who know where families are coming from.

Some of the most important times in a family's life are the times of "sacred play," times when they pause, even momentarily, to remember that there is more going on in the kitchen, the living room, the bedroom, and the backyard than just what meets the eye. At such times, families know that the God of the family is thick in the air.

# ESSAY:
# FAMILY AS SACRAMENT

### *MAUREEN GALLAGHER*

*Familiaris Consortio* uses the word sacrament in the narrowly defined sense of seven sacraments. However, there are some theological underpinnings in the document which allow us to develop a thesis that the family itself is a sacrament, and that it celebrates its sacramentality within itself and within the larger Christian community.

*Familiaris Consortio* calls the laity to interpret temporal realities in the light of Christ and to offer their unique and irreplaceable authentic discernment to the larger church (FC 5). The document also refers to the rich understanding and full integration of the mystery of Christ in their lives (FC 9). The rich understanding that families can offer the larger church emerges from a self-understanding that they are indeed a fundamental sacrament and they do indeed celebrate sacramentality within their experience of family.

To develop this idea, I shall present an understanding of sacrament that is a framework for the thesis, examine family life in the light of their understanding of sacrament, and finally, examine the document to determine how its theological understanding is congruent with the idea of family as sacrament.

## SACRAMENTALITY

In creating the world is permeated by God's grace. The very core of the world is graced by God's presence. The celebration of this fact is the heart of sacramentality. Grace is not something the Church gives when one performs rituals correctly. Grace is a gift from God—God's self-communication which is present whether it is accepted by people or not. Karl Rahner points out:

> This grace is not a particular phenomenon occurring parallel to the rest of human life but simply the ultimate depth of everything the spiritual creature does. When he realizes himself—when he laughs and cries, accepts responsibility, loves, lives and dies, stands up for truth, breaks out of preoccupation with self to help the neighbor, hopes against hope, cheerfully refuses to be embittered by the stupidity of daily life, keeps silent not so that evil festers in his heart but so that it does there—when in a word, man lives as he would like to live, in opposition to his selfishness and to the despair that always assails him. This is where grace occurs, because all this leads man into the infinity and victory that is God. (Rahner 97)

Grace is more perfectly manifested in Jesus who lived his life of ordinariness (which is comparable to ours) in an extraordinary manner. Because he accepted the presence and love of God, he was able to see his life differently. He saw more than meets the eye. As Teilhard de Chardin writes: "By reason of creation and even more than incarnation, nothing is profane for those who know how to see." How did Jesus see his life? Jesus saw a purpose or meaning in the ordinary. This distinctive way of seeing made the ordinary extraordinary. This seeing was the recognition of God's presence, of ultimate meaning in ordinary events. Jesus not only was the incarnation of God in human life, he saw incarnation all around him. He took as his mission the initiation of others into the incarnational mysteries of God. He used parables to say, "see differently;" he accented his words with visible signs of invisible reality.

We have described grace as the self-giving of God to the world and demonstrated that grace is epitomized in Jesus and his life of the ordinary made new by seeing anew. Another aspect of grace, which is at the heart of sacramentality, is the communal nature of grace. Because of the social nature of reality experienced by human beings, we cannot discuss grace only in relationship to individuals. Individuals always exist in relationship with others. Grace is interrelational insofar as individuals are in solidarity with the human race.

In order to understand Christian sacraments then, we need to include an awareness of Jesus' relationships to the community. Recognizing the specialness of their brother Jesus, the early disciples saw him as a person for God and about God. Their imagination was captured by the vision Jesus had of how things could be. After the death and resurrection of Jesus, the disciples wanted to pursue the vision he had of the Godliness of the world, which was their own graced existence. In a very real sense, the early Christians saw Jesus as the sacrament of encounter with God—the sign of God's Word and deed present in their everyday experience. God had graced their lives, given their lives a focus, a purpose, a reason for living—the greatest sign of this was Jesus himself.

The early Christians saw the presence of God's grace in Jesus and celebrated this first and foremost when they shared a meal together. There they recalled the presence of the Lord in their lives. They shared food and wine and recalled the events of Jesus' life. In doing this they evoked Jesus' very presence with them. They used their ordinary rituals and saw them in a new way.

The uniqueness of the Judeo-Christian faith lies in its experience and celebration of God's presence in life experiences. The biblical notion of faith always rooted faith in human experience. It was not an abstract, intellectual understanding of God's presence. Faith was seen as a force of life. People were rooted in faith. Grace was not a holy addition to life, but the core of life.

Sacraments grew out of the experiences of human life. Sacraments became events which the Christian community used to transform the ordinariness of human life, live it out in slow motion as a ritual, and in so doing come to a new realization of God's presence in the fabric of daily existence. The rituals that in the course of events became known as sacraments were not to make life automatically holy; rather, they pointed to the holiness which was inherent in a faith-filled existence and celebrated this awareness of inherent holiness communally.

Sacraments help people to be aware of the Godliness of life. They point to the extraordinary in the ordinary. They say there's "more than meets the eye" in birth, in death, in nurturing, in healing, in forgiving, in working through vocational pursuits, in growing through relationships, in helping one another cope with the realities of life.

The essential underlying theological concepts of sacramentality relate to: 1) God's self-communication with the world; 2) the recognition and acceptance of this in the ordinary events of life which is the task of faith; 3) the celebration of this grace within the community.

This concept of sacramentality is basic to any defined idea of Christian sacraments. Otherwise, Christian sacraments stand in danger of being understood in a way that borders on magic or in a manner that gives identity only to the clergy at the expense of the community.

## FAMILY LIFE AND SACRAMENTALITY

We have established that one of the primary reasons for doing sacraments is to recognize and celebrate the holiness in daily experience. Where can we find the power of God? In the family. Where can we see the "more than meets the eye" dimension of human experience? In the family. Where do we see people coming together in search of a purpose for living? In the family.

Theologians consider Jesus the primary sacrament of God's encounter with humanity (Schillebeeckx). Jesus by word and action made God's presence and care known. Jesus is truly a sacrament. Taken from another aspect, the Church is considered a sacrament because the Church by word and action manifests God's presence and proclaims the God dimensions interwove in life's experiences. The family can also be considered a sacrament. The family by word and deed manifests God's presence and leads its members to see the holiness which is part of everyday existence. For children, their primary experience of God is in their families. Whether in single parent or two parent families, children can know of

God's care because they experience parental acceptance; they know of God's nurture because they know parental nurture; they can know of God's steadfastness because they experience parental steadfastness. The same is true of forgiveness, healing, and affirmation of many kinds.

Not only is God's presence made known to children through at least one parent, but children themselves become the signs of God to parents. Co-creation is of itself an experience of Godliness. It doesn't have to be explained, nor does it have to be the focus of theology. Birth can be an ecstatic experience, an experience of the transcendent.

Even if one were to isolate particular events in family life, one would find that many of these parallel what we know as the seven sacraments. For instance, a series of events initiate children into adulthood: from teaching a child how to tie shoes to how to drive a car, there is constant calling forth and affirmation by the family. In fact, family life is full of initiation rituals which say to the person "we love you" or "we're glad you're here." Not only do parents initiate children into adulthood, but children initiate parents into the various challenges of parenthood. Initiation, affirmation, and accomplishment rituals (such as birthday parties, mortgage burnings, rituals related to losing teeth, obtaining a driver's license, and making the team) in a real sense flesh out the baptism and confirmation celebrated by the larger community. Family rituals such as these are family sacraments if they are recognized for their inherent value and seen in relationship to growth and development in Christian faith.

Nurturing is another basic ingredient of family life which is sacramental. Nurturing is seen on many levels: physical, psychological, emotional, and spiritual. One needs to be nurtured well at home before one can understand the community's celebration of Eucharist. Nurturing at home is in a real sense First Eucharist. The community of the family is the first sign of God's nourishment. Parents provide the first sacramental celebrations when they help children to see the "more than" just tangible food which makes up family meals.

Healing and forgiveness are also part of the "weft and warp" of family existence. Brokenness is often first experienced in family relationships. Reconciliation binds families together and helps them grow in relationships which affect the larger community.

Without belaboring this, we have pointed to the inherent holiness in family life and its sacramental celebration in the daily life of families. So, then, to return to the claim made at the beginning of this paper, does *Familiaris Consortio* allow for such an interpretation of the sacramentality of family life?

## FAMILIARIS CONSORTIO

The theology of sacramentality and family life which has been highlighted above is implicit in the theology which underlies *Familiaris Consortio*. I state this for the following reasons:

**First:** the theology of grace which underlies sacramental theology as described by Rahner earlier in the paper ("When a person laughs, cries, accepts responsibility, loves, lives...this is where grace occurs") is congruent with a theology of grace implicit in the document. An example of this is seen in relationship to grace and the building of the family community.

> All members of the family, each according to his or her own gift, have the grace and responsibility of building day by day the communion of persons, making the family "a school of deeper humanity": This happens where there is care and love for the little ones, the sick, the aged; where there is mutual service every day; when there is sharing of goods, of joys and of sorrows. (FC 21)

Furthermore, the document quoting Paul VI states that within a family "all members evangelize and are evangelized" (FC 39). Quoting the Second Vatican Council, *Familiaris Consortio* says that "By virtue of this sacrament [marriage], as spouses fulfill their conjugal and family obligations they are penetrated with the spirit of Christ, who wills their whole lives..." (FC 56). These and other similar examples point to an understanding of grace which pervades all of life.

**Second:** the family is called the "domestic church" (FC 21), repeating and citing the term used for the family in the Second Vatican Council document *Lumen Gentium*. The family is also called the "church in miniature" (FC 49), a concept the document introduces by saying, "the Christian family constitutes a specific revelation and realization of ecclesial communion, and for this reason too, it can and should be called, 'the domestic church'" (FC 21). Implicit in the idea of family being called church is the concept of family being sacrament or sign of the presence of Jesus. As church is a sacrament, so the family, as domestic church, is a sacrament. And just as the church celebrates sacraments in the community, so does the family ritualize its gifts, its ups and downs, its brokenness, its giftedness. It celebrates its relationships. It experiences life everyday; at certain times such as birthdays, parties, Sunday dinners or brunches, it take life in slow motion so its members can come to new realizations, new awarenesses of what they mean to each other. At such times families take their raw experiences, make them significant and celebrate them. This is the heart of sacramentality (Guzie). So I propose that by saying the family is "domestic church" the document is implying the family is sacrament.

**Third:** the notion of community which is integral to sacramental life is also critical to family life. The document states:

> Conjugal communion constitutes the foundation on which is built the broader communion of the family...This communion is rooted in the natural bonds of flesh and blood and grows to its specifically human perfection with the establishment and maturing of the still deeper and richer bond of the spirit: The love that animates the interpersonal relationships of the different members of the family constitutes the interior strength that shapes and animates the family communion and community. (FC 21)

A large amount of psychological research points to family as the first community or system where values are passed on. It is in the family where basic identity is usually assumed. It is the family who gives us saints by initiating and nourishing its members into Christian life. The community assembled for Eucharist is a major sign of the presence of the Lord. So also, the family community is a sign of the presence of the Lord.

While family is the most basic of communities, it is not a community unto itself. It needs to interact with and through other families and individuals and groups. The larger church community calls and challenges individual families to celebrate their identity and to grow through relationships with others beyond individual family membership. The document promotes families working with other families (FC 72). It sees the tasks of such relationships as fostering a sense of solidarity with other families, as favoring a life-style inspired by Gospel values, and as stimulating people to perform works of charity for one another.

At this point the importance of the family celebrating its sacramental dimension within the larger community needs to be recognized. In developing the notion of the sacramental dimension of family life, I am neither negating nor diminishing the importance of the celebrating of sacraments in the larger church community. Both are needed. Sacramental life is a two-sided coin: one side focuses on the family relationships; the other, on the larger community. Each nurtures the other. One without the other is incomplete.

In fact, if the sacramental dimension of life is not recognized in the family, it is probably inadequately understood or misunderstood as celebrated in the seven sacraments of the Catholic Christian Church. If sacramentality is only seen in the family community, the family's potential for growth is inhibited and the possibility of stagnation increases. It may be impoverished because it will not be nourished by the richness of the traditions of the larger church community.

**Fourth:** the sacramental dimension of the family can be seen precisely in its reciprocal relationship to the larger church community. The document addresses two patterns of relationships between church and family. At one point it talks about the family enriching the larger church community:

Inspired and sustained by the new commandment of love, the Christian family welcomes, respects and serves every human being, considering each one in his or her dignity as a person and as a child of God.

It should be so especially between husband and wife and within the family through a daily effort to promote a truly personal community, initiated and fostered by an inner communion of love. This way of life should then be extended to the wider circle of the ecclesial community of which the Christian family is a part.

Thanks to love within the family, the Church can and ought to take on a more homelike or family dimension, developing a more human and fraternal style of relationships. (FC 64)

At another point *Familiaris Consortio* speaks of the church proclaiming the good news to the family and challenging the family to develop its full potential for sacramentality:

Christians also have the mission of proclaiming with joy and conviction the good news about the family, for the family absolutely needs to hear ever anew and to understand ever more deeply the authentic words that reveal its identity, its inner resources and the importance of its mission in the city of God and in that of man. (FC 86)

This dual relationship is further alluded to:

To the extent in which the Christian family accepts the Gospel and matures in faith, it becomes an evangelizing community...

...the future of evangelization depends in a great parton the church of the home. (FC 52)

In summary, the family and the Church have an interdependent relationship as they participate in the mission of Jesus.

# CONCLUSION

Implicit in *Familiaris Consortio*, then, is the notion that the family is sacramental and celebrates its sacramentality within itself and within the larger community. In summary:

1. Grace is seen as permeating all life (FC 21, 39, 56).
2. The family is recognized as the "domestic church" (FC 21, 49, 52), thus implying participation in the sacramental dimension of Catholic Christianity.
3. Holiness is inherent in family life (FC 21). This is congruent with the church's theological understanding of sacramentality.
4. The family is seen to operate as a community of system (FC 50). Community is an essential theological symbol of sacramentality.
5. Family and the larger church community are seen in a reciprocal relationship. This, in the context outlined above, implies that the larger church community is enriched by the sacramentality of the family and that the family is nurtured by the holiness present in the larger church community (FC 64, 86, 50).

**WORKS CITED**

Guzie, Tad. *The Book of Sacramental Basics*. New York: Paulist Press, 1981.

Rahner, SJ, Karl. "How to Receive A Sacrament and Mean It." *Theology Digest* 19. 3 (Autumn): 97.

Schillebeeckx, OP, Edward. *Christ the Sacrament of the Encounter with God*. New York: Sheed and Ward, 1963.

4

# ESSAY:
# ROLE OF RITUAL
# AND CELEBRATION

## *GERTRUD MUELLER NELSON*

## "PRECESSION"

Some years ago, I spent an afternoon caught up in a piece of
sewing I was doing. The waste basket near my sewing machine
was filled with scraps of fabric cut away from my project. This
basket of discards was a fascination to my daughter, Annika,
who, at the time, was still three years old. She rooted through
the scraps searching out the long bright strips of cloth,
collected them to herself, and went off. When it had been
silent too long, I took a moment to check on her and tracked
her whereabouts to the back garden. I found her there, sitting
in the grass with a long pole she had gotten from the garage.
She was fixing the scraps to the top of the pole with great
sticky wads of tape. Mothers sometimes ask foolish questions,
and I asked one. I asked her what she was doing. Without
taking her eyes from her work she said, "I'm making a banner
for a precession [sic]. I need a precession so that God will
come down and dance with us." With that, she solemnly lifted
her banner to flutter in the wind, and slowly we got up to
dance.

I don't think that Annika was a particularly precocious
toddler. I think, rather, she was doing what three-year-olds do
when left to their natural and intuitive religious sense, and I
was simply fortunate to hear and see what she was about.
Mothers often hear wonderful things from their youngsters. We
are the anthropologists, if you will, and our children are the
exotic primitives who also happen to be under foot. This small

primitive allowed me to witness a holy moment, and I learned all over again how strong and real is that sense of wonder that children have—how innate and easy their way with the sacred. She had all the necessary elements for a religious ritual: a thing and an action. Here, religion was child's play. I had to wonder what happens in our development that as adults we become a serious folk, uneasy in our relationship with God, out of touch with the mysteries we knew in childhood, restless, empty, searching to regain a sense of awe and a way, once again, to "dance with God."

Indeed, I had to wonder what happens to our children on their way to adulthood that they become *too quickly* alienated from their religious sense and become the small monsters that even a Thomas Merton had observed. The modern child, he noted, may early in his or her existence have natural inclinations toward spirituality. The child "may have imagination, originality, a simple and individual freshness of response to reality and even a tendency to moments of thoughtful silence and absorption." All these tendencies, however, are soon destroyed by the dominant culture. The child "becomes a yelling, brash, false little monster, brandishing a toy gun and dressed up like some character he has seen on television. His head is filled with inane slogans, songs, noises, explosions, statistics, brand names, menaces, ribaldries and cliches." Then, when the child goes to school, he learns "to verbalize, to rationalize, to pose, to make faces like an advertisement, to need a car and in short, to go through life with an empty head, conforming to others like himself, in togetherness" (Merton).

I think we can say that our "fall from innocence" is a fact of the human condition. But I think that as parents and teachers, we have to consider our own role in *shoving* children out of the garden of their original innocence too soon, too harshly, without any tools for understanding the frantic actions that send each one in hungry search for an unknown and unnamed entity. For it is also a fact of the human condition that, once banished from the garden, *we never stop longing and seeking to be made whole again.*

## KNOWLEDGE VS. MEANING

Life's tasks of learning to think and compare, to sort and choose began with our first taste of "knowledge of good and evil," and for that fruit we have developed a great appetite. It is, in fact, knowledge that changes our innocent relationship with God. And we spend the rest of our days circling the garden of our original innocence, yearning to find our way back in.

Unless we become again as little children—but as little children who know their own hearts—we cannot enter the kingdom of heaven. Our way back to a connection with God is through the profound experience of our humanity. When we live artfully the mysteries of our humanness, we will know our hearts; we will see beyond the obvious to the mysteries hidden in the ordinary. For the route we choose to the kingdom is marked with the mysteries of the human condition: births and deaths, joys and sufferings, peak experiences and pitfalls. And when we are struck with the *meaning* of our most human experiences, we are most closely connected with the divine.

So then, it is in the mysteries of our humanity—of our human developmental cycles—of our everyday feelings, our pains, failures and triumphs, meetings and partings, birthing, living, dying and rising again where we may suddenly recognize God, and these are the occasions which we encircle, compelled to *do* something in celebration and recognition and invitation to the transcendent.

The Church in her poetic aspect—which has always been there for us and has always been centered in the cycles of our human development—nourishes us through rite and symbol, through rhythmic repetition, through liturgical action. The poetic Church celebrates our cycles and seasons, inviting us to be fully human, asking us to see and engage and feel the touch and taste and be aware and grow and be transformed. Through our celebration of the Church cycle, through custom and liturgy, through sacrament and sacramental, through rituals and holy folklore and holy play, the personal experiences which make up our daily lives are affirmed and made sacred.

Furthermore, this creative and poetic Church helps us to pay full attention to what the dominant culture would have us deem ordinary and commonplace. Rituals and symbols use the ordinary things in life. We have to remind ourselves daily to preserve for our children the holiness of everyday things. We have to develop an art of living, a sacramental mentality, for the transcendent is disclosed in what is wonderfully simple and familiar—indeed, in bread, wine, fire, ash, earth, water, oil, tears, seeds, songs, feastings and fastings, pains and joys, bodies and thoughts, regressions and transformations. Christian ritual draws its action from what is most human in us more than from heady ideas from theology. Liturgy is not an idea; it is not knowledge dressed up in gestures. It is simply up and *doing* in bodily action what the heart already knows.

It is the role of the creative teacher and the thoughtful parent to nurture the natural religious sense of their children, and their own inner, forgotten child, I might add. We must protect them as long as we can from the clamor of the world and what it tells them they need to buy for their fulfillment. We must help them to know their own soul and provide or perfect the rituals and forms that will touch the places of life's mysteries and give them back meaning—not a sentimentalized meaning but a meaning that they will never outgrow.

A return to the creative function of the Church, its myth, rites, and symbols, is a step forward in this nurturance. It builds on our natural sense of what is holy and returns us to the sacred when we have become flooded and numbed with the clamors of the world. Rites and celebrations provide the ultimate religion lesson: *a recognition that God is revealed in our humanness.*

## SO WHEN WAS THE LAST TIME THAT GOD REVEALED HIMSELF TO YOU?

I live near the beach, and often I watch how children respond to the ocean. I watched, once, how three children stood with considerable awe before the grand ocean as it rose up in huge waves and repeatedly crashed onto the beach. The powerful water was not to be rushed into lightly or with abandon. They regarded the whole drama in silence as they clung to their mother's legs. Then with a little daring, the oldest launched an age-old ritual which we can all remember having performed ourselves and which we can see repeated over and over again wherever there are small children at the beach. The child turned her back on what was too awesome, and she began to dig a hole. Her brothers joined her. They dug and scooped the sand until they had a sizeable hollow, and slowly they allowed something of the great sea to enter and fill their hole. It became their mini-sea. It was a body of water that they could easily encompass and control. In time, they stomped in the puddle and splashed with abandon in a way that they were not yet willing to do in the surf. Then the surf rose higher and swished into their hole, wiping out one of its walls. With a delicious mixture of thrill and horror, they repeatedly rebuilt their walls, and the ocean repeatedly washed them down. Their manageable sea always let in something of the unmanageable. This was a game that they were able to play for a very long time. For them, it was a religious experience. They had created a hole to catch something of the transcendent.

For us, this story is the paradigm for ritual making. Ritual and ceremony are the container we create to hold something of a mystery. We all seek the container that can carry the touch of God for us. It is natural to us as human beings to make rituals because we are, by nature, religious people.

## THE SYMPTOMATIC WAY

Even in this very secular world that no longer centers itself in the religious, our quest for "something more" cannot be denied. Today, we are not likely to take our children on pilgrimage to visit holy shrines and the bones of saints or the tunic of Mary. *But we all still go on pilgrimage*—we still have our meccas. Disneyland may be such a "holy land" where God is rendered Mickey Mouse. Our religious nature is still at the root of who we have become. We may think that over time we have shrugged off all manner of "empty" religious rituals and ceremonies, but it turns out that we have only created a vacuum, a void which is quickly filled either by offerings from the secular world which knows our hunger and can profit from it or by unconscious rituals we put in place of the ancient rituals whose meaning has faded.

We are not as free to choose or not choose our rituals and symbolic behavior as we may think. Actually, our only choice is between conscious rituals and unconscious ones—those which enrich, dignify, and enliven our lives and interactions and those which enslave us, which deaden life and block us from deep human relationship and meaning.

Without a way to consciously feed and express our basic religious nature, we allow our religious experiences to enter through the back door in the manner of our habits, our fears, our neuroses, and symptoms. In place of the periodic, holy fast, for instance, we have become slaves to our perennial diets. In exchange for "carrying our cross" in the constructive suffering that every life requires, we complain of low-back pain. The old taboos from which we think we are freed crop up as new varieties of superstitions for which we take another vitamin. The neurotic is religious material done unconsciously. Neurosis is the modern parody of religious and is the consequence of our lost orientation to the sacred.

When we recognize the holy nature of the moment and understand the meaning of a given experience, we can make it holy with a ritual. If we don't honor that moment with a conscious ritual, an unconscious solution will come forward to deal with what we are trying to face.

## GOING TO BED

Let me give you an example—putting a small child to bed. Mother is in the kitchen mashing avocado for a dip and watching the oven so that the meringue on the top of her pie doesn't burn. Guests are about to arrive, and she is caught up in making her preparations for dinner. Dad is on a ladder outside the front door replacing a light bulb. Small Teddy has been sent off to bed with shouted reminders to brush his teeth, not eat the toothpaste, and wash behind his ears. Then Mother rushes in for a quick hug, tucks him in, and turns out the light.

Any one of us observing this scene knows already that this isn't going to work. Bedtime is a very big transition for a small child to make. Transitions are fraught with uncertainty and danger. It is difficult to give oneself over to the darkness when the primordial fear of being abandoned or left to wild beasts is still an inner reality. But Mother hurries down the hall to her lemon meringue pie, and, of course, she hears the patter of little feet right behind her. "But I want to see if the company has come, but I only want to kiss you, but I don't like it all dark." So Mother hustles Teddy back into bed, not once, but several times while Teddy with an ingenuity that astounds, whips up a bedtime ritual for himself that he hopes will bring him a little security. This ritual includes another hug for Daddy, the light put on in the bathroom, a night light installed in his room. He badly wants a bedtime story, and if Mother's not game, he'd be glad to tell a long-winded one himself. He needs half a zoo of stuffed animals tucked into bed with him along with three of his favorite trucks. Mother finally flies to her meringue pie which she discovers smoking and black in the oven. And from the hall, we hear Teddy: "I need a drink!"

From this common experience, we can see why most of the religious rituals that we know are centered around times of transition. Teddy's parents would have far greater success with their son if they would first understand that Teddy is not being a bad boy. He is afraid. His hard-won daylight consciousness is difficult to give up to the darkness without some protection and comfort. Teddy, because he is still a child, doesn't have the skills to devise a *conscious ritual* for himself, but he *is* devising a ritual—an unconscious one—to deal with the mysteries of the dark. Wise parents will have created a comforting routine for putting this little boy to bed, the child having provided some of the ingredients for this ritual. It will be a ritual that is both practical—we get bathed and brushed—and reassuring. This ritual will be basically the same every night. It may include a retelling of the events of the day, a story, and certainly night prayers. A blessing, perhaps with the Easter water brought home from the Vigil service, will guard against fear and give strength. A kiss, a firm and certain "good night," and Teddy knows that now it is safe to go to sleep.

## ADULT BEDTIME

Without conscious rites to close the day, even the enlightened adult can come up against some curious compulsions, habits, or superstitious behaviors which are an attempt to close the day and guard against the powerful and unknown elements of the unconscious. Imagine the adult who goes to bed. Have you ever settled into bed and then wondered if you locked the back door? You get up to check again. While you're up anyway, maybe you'll fix yourself a little cup of something hot to help you sleep. You make another trip to the bathroom, check in the mirror again—those crows feet around the eyes need a dab of cream. You crawl into bed—blast! Did you turn the gas off after you heated your milk? Better check. You pad down the hall again. It was off, but you can never be too sure. Now, back to bed. You slip in. You pull up the covers. You settle down. Ah! But you forgot to close the closet door! Unclear about what the fear is and distracted from a more meaningful way to close the day, you are driven through your routines until you finally sleep.

No wonder that the Benedictine Rule offers clear, consistent, comforting, disciplined ways to deal with bedtime—in fact, with every transition of the day.

The most important ceremonies in our human cycles have to do with transitions, helping us to get from one level to the next. During transitions, we are vulnerable and in danger. Like the creature who has outgrown an old skin and can wear it no longer, we shed what is no longer fitting. But thus exposed, we are in a state of crisis; we feel soft and unprotected and unsure of the future "skin" that is still unknown to us. In times of transition, we are tempted to turn back to our old ways: these are at least warm and familiar to us; the new is frightening and unfamiliar. But we know how unsuccessful our attempts at crawling back into an old and worn-out skin can be.

Colin Turnbull, in his marvelous accounting of the Mbuti people of Zaire, passes along to us their understanding of the dangers in transition. The Mbuti see the person as being in the center of a sphere. In moving from here to there, the sphere moves too and offers protection. If movement in time or space is too sudden or vehement, we risk the danger of reaching the boundaries of the sphere too quickly, before the center has time to catch up. When this happens, persons become *wazi-wazi* or disoriented and unpredictable. If they pierce through the safe boundaries of the sphere into the other world, they risk letting in something else which takes their place. If the Mbuti know of and guard against such violent and sudden motion—and that without the experience of automobiles or jet planes—what do we, the so-called civilized people of the world, know of our transitions in space and time? I think we are a whole society in a state of *wazi-wazi*, beside ourselves, possessed by imposter selves.

Even though most of our everyday transitions may be small ones—going to bed or getting up in the morning, driving to work or coming home at night—we know them to be powerful the minute we recognize the agitation and the pent up feelings that we carry at those moments. Transitions are by their very nature difficult and psychologically and spiritually dangerous because we are tempted to regress. That is the reason I don't like to talk to anyone in the morning until I have had my first cup of coffee. That is why my shoulders ache while I fight my way through traffic as I drive home at night. That is why I find it so difficult to deal with the pile of mail that waits for me inside the door as I step into the house. My own children have pointed out to me that when I return home after an extended trip away, I head straight for the kitchen which I seem to hold as my personal territory and begin to wipe counters and sweep the floor. Irritated because the kitchen has actually been *used* by others during my absence, the imposter mother has arrived and bustles around giving orders. And my children comment: "Mother's riding her broom again."

Of course, there are transitions to be dealt with on a grand scale too: birthing and dying are the ultimate transitions, and rebirth and our final resurrection are actually what all this small stuff is about. We are practicing at our ultimate transitions and final transformation by muddling through the "terrible twos" of our own unsung, mid-life crisis.

It is appropriate to pay attention to the feelings that we go through at the great moments of transition in our lives. These are opportunities to point up, with consciousness, the change, the transformation, that we are invited to make. Here, through ritual or ceremony, we find courage and communal or individual support. A ritual or a celebration of the moment will invite a feeling discharge and offer safety to the person at risk. While we shed our old ways and embrace a new way, a ceremony will make the sacred experience taste both bitter and sweet. We rejoice at weddings because we are witness to a new and profound beginning, but we might also cry, because we are witness to the end of an era. The first day of school may be exciting and hold great promise. The first day of school may also fill one with fear and feelings of loss. I know a school that has the most delightful celebrations for Valentine's Day. But in their wisdom it is not all lace and ice cream. The children have special presentations and discussions about their own friendships—about social cliques, about gossip, about feelings of rejection or inferiority. Rites are meant to engage both halves of the truth, the dark and the light, because a half truth is sentimentality or a lie. Good ceremony continually deals with both sides of a question in order to arrive at a place that can contain them both.

In the classroom, in the parish, it is the creative teacher and planner who knows that we need forms and rituals and ceremonies within which to express ourselves and be nourished and safe. The *art* of making this form a form which nourishes is far more important than the other administrative services that often bog us down. Ritual making and ceremony require leaders who are not afraid to recognize their talent or insight and are willing to step forward to use it. Before we can plan the larger liturgies, we must be sensitive to the minor cycles, the daily moments that need recognition, consciousness, and an artful ritual.

When I taught at an East Coast school in the days of its founding, it was easy to recognize that our administrators were so caught in the throes of administration and the constantly changing aspects of a new school—in daily re-inventions of the wheel—that I offered to create a service which we then called "All-School Celebrations." The celebrations were meant to make some thing in our lives certain and unchanging. They centered around the issues of transition and high feeling—anger, fear, excitement, disappointment, success, envy, joy. In time, these celebrations or simple rituals covered everything from how we greeted the children at the door each morning or dismissed them in the afternoon, to how the whole school prayed and sang together each morning. They affected how the teachers ate together in the lounge, how we relieved tensions or helped the children to get rid of extra energy or fear: rituals that engage feelings fully and then discharge them. They covered the basketball games between the children and the staff, how we prepared the children and brought them to Mass, how we celebrated Advent as a whole school or prepared a class for first Eucharist, how we dealt with the deaths of some members in our community, or how we greeted the birth of a student's new sibling.

We carefully studied our attraction to the power of symbol—from birthday cakes to school awards and diplomas. We included many symbols of transformation. We made jam and churned butter. We planted gardens and tended a compost pile. We learned that we could make an art of any of life's tasks from washing the chalk boards to mending the stone fences. We aligned our school year with the Church year and drew from her sacraments and sacramentals. We looked to anthropology and folklore for further richness and ideas for dealing with the human events of a school community in formation. It was gratifying to visit that school 20 years later and find some things still firmly entrenched as part of the character and identity of that school. If you are a teacher and have devised something that is powerfully satisfying, keep it and perfect it and spread it around the school. For "school spirit" is not to be found or formed only on the playing field. School spirit is God's Spirit as expressed in our creative approach to human history, human situations.

## HOME RITUALS

In the same way, in a family, parents need to provide a structure and form that safeguards and feeds all of its members. There are the daily cycles to pay attention to, the yearly cycles, and there is the human cycle, common to all of us. A birthday celebration, beyond the birthday candles, can engage the whole family in this moment of personal history. The birthday child loves to hear the story of how she was born—every wonderful detail. She wants to hear, every year, how it was -30° that night and Papa had to push the car to get started. She wants to know about the baby clothes her mother packed in her bags before her trip to the hospital. The family looks at the old baby books, and the birthday child sits at the head of the table while all present take a turn to say what is special about her and what they like so much about her. The birthday child has a chance to talk about the great events of the past year and her hopes and fears for the year ahead.

In our house, birthday children, to help them engage this day as a developmental step, are given two envelopes. One is marked "Privilege": "Now that you are eight years old you may ride your bicycle as far as Maple Street!" The other envelope is marked "Responsibility": "Now that you are eight years old, you must help the household by scrubbing the bathroom sinks every Saturday morning before you go off to play." The beauty of that one is that the distinction between "privilege" and "responsibility" wasn't made in the early years. I remember a wail coming out of the bathroom from my daughter Sara when she was about eight. "Someone already cleaned the sink and it was my *privilege*!" At 16, the envelope may hold a key to the family car, and the responsibility covers the task of a periodic oil change. Such a ceremony allows the child to see life as process and developmental stages.

In families, we need to re-evaluate the rituals we already have and discern if they are worthy and conscious of whatever mystery we are trying to engage. Mealtime in the American family is in a state of disrepair. How ever can we understand the Eucharist if the family meal does not allow us to "know him in the breaking of the bread?" We need to devise ways of marking important moments—little moments and grand ones. We need some private rites of passage for our children—not as powerful, perhaps, as communal, tribal rites of other cultures but better than the school proms and drinking parties that our culture offers. We need ways to leave home in our youth and ways to enter retirement as we grow old. We need ways to prepare for new life and ways to face our own death. At its core, a rite or ceremony points us, through our human experiences, to the transcendent. Through rites, we raise what is happening to us to a level of conscious awareness, and in doing so we actively seek to be transformed.

# THE CYCLE OF THE CHURCH YEAR

Since we've considered our daily, human experiences, it may not come as a surprise that the feasts and seasons of the Church year correspond closely to and are the grace-filled, practice fields of our personal cycles. Advent celebrates the marriage of heaven to earth and our anticipation of the birth of the God-man. It connects us to every sort of waiting and pregnancy that our personal lives might ever know, from waiting for the bus to healing the split between what is every day and earthly and the inspiration of spirit. Christmas brings us a Saviour and new hope. The mystery of the Incarnation makes all matter holy because God found the human body, and barnyard, and the company of peasants the perfect setting for his Son. Lent offers us the opportunity to suffer and to die to our false selves. Through the Lord's own passion, we learn to understand the sufferings that weave in and out of our daily lives—the necessary crosses that are prerequisite to the glorious transformation of the Easter mysteries.

From the feasts and mysteries of the Church year, we draw the sort of nourishment that is the only antidote I know to the false, poisoning versions of life and meaning concocted and served up by our consumer culture. By celebrating through the structure of the Church, we actually are given the forms we need to become whole, and we are given the formulas to make whole every human experience. This effort requires our rediscovery of the themes which the cycle of the Church calendar offers us and the application of our creative imagination to the rites and folk customs already available. Then, through the celebration of the sacred mysteries, we will find new meaning in the inexplicable and a worthy container for what we realize in our hearts. That means that in the parish community, in the school, and in the family, if we are honest about living the themes of the Church calendar, we must come to know and touch and be touched by the mysteries of that season.

## ADVENT

Using Advent as a case in point, we immerse ourselves in the spirit of the season—together with our immediate community and with all the ages of people who have gone before us and will come after us—to *wait* and fully engage what it means to be spiritually pregnant. Waiting is something we all hate to do. We hate it so much that we have invented instant coffee, plastic grass, Concorde airplanes, and "hold music" for the telephone.

But waiting is something we already know as a reality in our lives. Much as we are tempted to fight against it, we know it to be a valuable fact of life. To pull the cake out of the oven too soon, simply because we can't wait any longer, only gives us a runny cake. Waiting is necessary, the vital ingredient to anything of quality or value: a ripened fruit, a healthy baby, a work of art, a reconciled relationship. It is also necessary to a healthy Christmas. Because we hate to wait, the commercial world urges us to jump the gun, and by the time Christmas actually comes we are sick of it all—the tree is dry, Santa Claus is old hat, and the new blouse is the wrong size. Somehow, the arrival of the new life has been aborted, and there is no healthy satisfying Christmas.

For this reason, I think it is the job of the parish and school community and caring parents to learn again the *art of waiting* and then to teach it. Waiting is not some punishment that the Church imposes on us, but rather it is the discipline that enhances our appreciation of life and makes it healthy. Advent invites us to underscore and understand with a new patience that very feminine state of being, waiting. Our masculine world wants to blast it away, and we see as progressive every device invented that eliminates what we have learned to see as time wasted. But studies show that the time saved is not necessarily time given back to us to live more humanly. We tend rather only to speed up our action and our busyness. Waiting is unpractical time, good for nothing, but mysteriously necessary for all that is becoming. Brewing, baking, simmering, fermenting, ripening, germinating, gestating are the feminine processes of becoming, and they are the symbolic states of being which belong in a life of value, *necessary to transformation*. Ultimately, the deep-seated chauvinism of our culture which despises this feminine element in life is well illustrated in our general inability to celebrate the season of Advent.

It is always surprising to me how many church schools and parishes—communities which should be the examples and inspiration to us all—offer Christmas programs during this sacred time of waiting. To use the excuse that we don't have the children over Christmas is to misunderstand our mission to teach the spirit of the liturgy. Advent as a time for preparation and anticipation is also a time filled with liturgical encouragement, folk customs, and Advent songs and carols. But none of these exercises in waiting make any sense if they are overlaid with Christmas decorations and parties. Even our efforts at gathering the greens and weaving our Advent wreath as symbol of our waiting and preparation is thus relegated to a meaningless gimmick or cute decoration.

## ADVENT WREATH AS SYMBOL

The Advent wreath, on the other hand, as a serious "outward sign" has a powerful symbolic function. For the power of symbol puts us directly in touch with a force or an idea by use of an image or an object. A "thing" can do that for us. But for that to happen, we have to get involved in it, in its making and using, in its fragrance and its light. Most of all, we have to remember that the Advent wreath was once a wagon wheel—a wheel *removed* and rendered *useless* and inactive. It is the sacrifice of an everyday object, taken for granted and ever rotating, now stopped and brought indoors as a sign of a different time, *sacred time*, a time to halt action and turn inward. The recovery of hope, in the year's darkest season, can only be accomplished when we have had the courage to stop and wait and engage fully in the winter of our dark longing. Then the symbolic reality of an Advent wreath has deep and penetrating power. It bridges the gulf between knowing and believing. It integrates mind and heart.

It is also important to remember that at the core of the major rituals that we choose or create for home and parish, it is wise to keep a character which is broader and richer and deeper than a too-narrow personal piety or a disjointed array of spontaneous actions and reactions. We use forms that carry to some extent a symbolic essence and that are rooted in the past, yet are living expression that have helped many people to know themselves and express themselves. A broad approach in the actions and words and objects we choose will, like good liturgy, transcend the private, the immediate, and connect us with the rest of humankind, giving a sense of unity and purpose that will not leave us caught in our own narrow world.

This broader approach is also important in creating family rituals. It is the difference between putting out marshmallows on the windowsill for Santa's elves rather than putting straws into the manger during Advent for good deeds done in preparation for the coming of the Child. When children grow up and express their spiritual independence and reject the narrow familiar realm, they will, if parents have grounded them in  scriptural language and a deep, spiritual heritage, find that meaning to be still available to them, and certain customs will continue to nourish and hold meaning for them. Sentimentality, poor taste, ugly forms, trite expressions, artificial greens, and fake snow do not hold over time. Rather, the oldest customs and traditions often hold the kind of richness which we need never outgrow. For this reason, we have to keep looking at and talking over the visual shape we give to the sacred world and its hidden events.

## CHRISTMASTIDE

Of course it is important to remember—with all the longing, the excitement, the counting of days, the anticipation, and happy preparations that we engage in while we await the coming of the Saviour—that we don't go through all that to celebrate for a single day. We celebrate all 12 days of Christmas, and there are folk customs for almost every one of those days that follow Christmas. In our parish, we end the season with a party on the Feast of Epiphany. It seems wonderfully appropriate for a school to welcome the children back from their long Christmas vacation with a grand closure of the season still to look forward to.

Some of the high points of our own parish celebration may serve as examples of how to celebrate Epiphany either on a small scale with the family or on a large scale with a parish community or school. The whole parish arrives, young and old, on the night before Epiphany or on the evening of Epiphany itself. We sing all the Christmas carols we know for the last time that season. We have three large cakes, one for the small children, one for the teenagers, and one for the adults. In each cake, a navy bean is hidden. Those who find the beans become kings, Casper, Melchior, and Balthazar, and are the royal representatives of their age groups. They are robed and crowned on the spot and cheered by their loyal subjects. Then accompanied by kazoos and horns, coffee-can drums and rattling car keys, the whole company of loyal subjects sings "We Three Kings" and follows their kings in procession into the gym—in our case, the church, because we have no other large space. A large star at the top of a pole is at the head of the procession and halts at a given place. Now the kings must embark on a wild Parcheesi game where the points of a star are spun and fate dictates the number of steps that they make take on their arduous journey toward Bethlehem—the creche at the altar. In our parish, we arrange a "living Bethlehem" and give a role to all the smaller children who are now dressed as Mary and Joseph, shepherds, and angels and are arranged and waiting at the foot of the altar.

The kings, waiting at the back of the church, move from one "stepping stone" to the next, and when they have used up their number of steps, they read the verdict under their feet. "You have forgotten to water your camels—go back to the oasis." "You have lost sight of the star; go back to square one." "Friendly shepherds point the way; go forward three steps." "Sandstorms are forecast; hole up for one turn." Field and fountain, moor and mountain, and finally they come to Herod's castle. They have a serious encounter with Herod who awaits them there. Herod is played by an adult who, in his own oily way, questions the kings to find out their motives for wanting to find the Child and asks them to return to him with information and directions. The whole assembly hisses at that one. But otherwise, cheering and clapping, each age group urges on their own king.

Last time, when things got very tense and close, it was marvelous to see St. Joseph, up front, drop his staff and start pounding his knees and shout, "Come on Balthazar! You can make it!" when it looked like his king was going to win. When all the kings finally arrive and the Bethlehem scene has settled down again into position, we hear the Gospel story of the Magi read to us once more, an echo of the Epiphany liturgy. Our pastor gives a little homily. Then every family is sent home with a piece of blessed chalk to mark the doorways of their homes in a special and old ceremony for the blessing of homes on Epiphany. It is a delightful way to act out the Gospel and to consider the journey on which we all find ourselves as we take two steps forward and one step back in our daily search for the Christ.

This communal celebration of the feast of Three Kings is just one example of how a community can end its Christmas celebrations with a true climax and head into the new year refreshed and sustained. It seems to be the perfect antidote to any possible after-Christmas blues. Variations of this celebration, if they cannot be carried off by your parish, are the perfect occasion for family and neighborhood celebrations. The last of the fruitcakes and cookies are served. A king or kings are elected with the fate of the bean-cake. The lintel over the door is blessed with the markings of the Three Kings and the date of the new year: 19 C + M + B + 92. And finally, the tree is taken down in ceremony and with reverent finality.

There are celebrations to follow in the coming months—one last fling at Mardi Gras precedes our Lenten fast. There are endless helps that encourage us to engage our fast and to be reconciled to one another. These cannot all be mentioned here, but there are many detailed examples in my book *To Dance with God*. It is right to remember that the liturgies of the Church year are enhanced and pointed up by our communal efforts. And community is enhanced and strengthened by our joint feasts and fasts.

While there are many, many more occasions to consider for celebrations during the Church year—unfortunately, we have not the space here—it seems right that we consider briefly the issue of our Easter celebrations.

## A COPTIC EASTER

A few years ago, a film on public television showed the Easter vigil services as they were celebrated in a Coptic church in Jerusalem. In the dead of night, hundreds of people gathered in the cathedral, and hundreds more collected outside the doors. They had all come along after a long and serious Lenten fast. Inside the church, tinder had been laid for the Easter fire. When the bishop arrived, he stood before the tinder and a hush fell over the crowd. They waited for the tinder to ignite. Coptic Christians claim that this happens by spontaneous combustion and only if the celebrant has prayed and properly fasted. When the tinder glowed and then burst into flame, a roar came from the crowd, and they cheered the new and holy fire. Then in the darkened church, the fire was passed from person to person. When it reached the doors, they were opened, and the fire was passed to the crowds outside. A new roar rose from those outside as they saw and accepted the holy fire.

## OUR EASTER

Our own Easter fires must have something of that same sacred, breathless, will-it-ignite quality about them. That is why the old rubrics require that the fire be lit from flint and steel. There has to be the breathless quality of chance, the realness of flame and fire passed amongst us, the cheers of relief and success. For that, we hear chanted *Lumen Christi!* We have that wonderful word *Alleluia*, that ritual cry of joy and relief which we have not heard for over six, Lenten weeks. For that we sing the *Gloria* and ring the church bells. Our church has no bells so everybody brings a bell from home. At the intonation of the *Gloria*, out come the muffled bells; then we ring them like mad—lots of little bells, some big bells, dinner gongs, even a cow bell. At that point we have to at least smile, and the children just laugh aloud.

A token fire, lit in a little bowl at the back of the church where no one hears or secs or smells it—flicked into existence quickly with the aid of lighter fluid and a cigarette lighter—is no archetypal fire. It has lost power. An *Alleluia* that has not been sung in a glorious number of ways all year then is denied, and pealed forth again in the midst of the Easter night, has lost impact and meaning.

## BURIAL OF THE ALLELUIA

I remember a time when I was preparing a class of children for Lent. All year at morning prayers, we had sung psalms and *Alleluias*. And now I explained that that cheerful word would be denied us. We wouldn't say or sing it even once for the six weeks of Lent. What could we do with that word so that it was out of our reach? The children, seated in a ring around me, began to chatter. Some made motions with their hands of pressing it down. "Bury it!" was one suggestion. "Yah! Bury it!" they agreed. Without knowing it, they were suggesting a ritual burial of the *Alleluia* that was indeed a known and common practice in other times and in other parts of the world. Given the chance, the children responded directly and simply from the collective unconscious. So we got out large sheets of paper and each wrote the word large and beautifully, every letter decorated with designs and flowers and joyful colors and signs of spring. We sang all the *Alleluias* we knew for the last time. Then they folded their papers and took these home, put them in jars and found a place in their garden to bury them until Easter.

This little ritual, which rose quite spontaneously from my students, almost backfired. It happened that two of the children, a brother and a sister, were out digging their holes when their father arrived home from work. He saw them burrowing amongst his daffodils, one in the front garden and one in the back, and he demanded to know what they were doing. The boy offered that they were burying a word—a word that he couldn't say any more—their teacher said so. "What word? Did you learn it from her?" "Sure, of course!" The girl wouldn't make the story any clearer. "It's a very special word and we're not going to say it, not until Easter and then..." But apparently by that time the father was in the house demanding an explanation from me on the phone. When I explained, he was not only relieved but delighted and resolved to join the children in a resurrection of the *Alleluia* on Easter morning as a part of the family egg-hunting ceremonies.

## DOING WITHOUT FIRE

In my parish, now, there are families who have made it a practice during the days from Good Friday to Easter, to do without fire, that is without anything that requires a flame, like cooked food. Some even give up hot showers so that when the sacred fire of the Easter night is kindled and blessed and praised and sung to, it can be brought home again by a candle in a jar. The holy fire is used to renew the pilot lights and kindle a fresh fire in the cleaned-out hearth. We learned that certain Native Americans, the Incas, and the ancient Chinese have such a festival in the spring, and they too receive a sacred fire from the shaman. The Incas, for instance, wait for their shaman to receive it. He catches it by means of a crystal directly from the Sun, then distributes it to every household that has been cold and dark and without cooked food for three days.

I can remember a blustery, rainy Easter night where parishioners had witnessed the successful lighting of the Easter fire against all odds. Once inside the church, we felt blessed and victorious with our little flames.

After services and after the Easter feastings and greetings were over, we all trekked out to our cars in a blowing rain trying to get our little flames as far as the car. Two young men approached us from the parking lot. They told us they'd gotten all the way to their van, and in slamming the door, their candle had gone out. They wanted to share in our flame and wanted to warn us that even closing the car door was a danger to getting our fire home successfully. We shared our flame, crept into our car, and, sure thing, when we closed the door—even though we were ever so careful—our candle went out!

The two young men had not driven off yet. They were sitting in their van watching to see how we would fare. Again, they shared their light with us, and we had to laugh with joy and satisfaction at our fire-light fraternity. As they drove off, the next family came knocking at our car window needing a light from our candle. We gave them a tip on how to close the car door and save the flame. Up and down the parking lot in the wind and the rain we heard the families laughing and calling out as flames went out and were rekindled. "Wow," said one of our kids. "This fire *is* magic! I know what you mean—you can give it away and you never lose; it only makes more." In the *Exsultet*, we had just sung "*A flame divided but undimmed*." And here, we were experiencing it in some very graphic way.

We also carry home the newly blessed water in a special bottle and use that water to bless our Easter foods the next morning. We save that water, in its very beautiful bottle, to use throughout the coming year: to bless those in the family who may be ill, or traveling, or taking an important exam. It blessed little children at bedtime. It blessed the new car, the seeds that go into the ground in the spring, the Advent wreath, the Christmas tree. Over and over, we are reminded of our baptism into this community of believers and of how our membership has an impact on everything that happens to us, no matter how everyday the situation. This is not superstition, not magic, but rather a rite to engage and heighten the awareness of the moment and call God's grace into the situation.

When the Church denies us something, like the use of *Alleluia*, or encourages a fast or when it asks us to wait during Advent, too often, for too long, we have viewed these periods of denial or longing as a punishment and as masochistic. In reality, we can come to see that periods of denial really help us to experience life's gifts with greater joy and awareness. I think that the Church, even though we have a tendency to forget this, is a great teacher of joy. Indeed, there is no crown without a cross. But this is the balance we must create in our lives.

It is in this spirit that we go forth to be true to the themes which the Church year offers us and which match and point up and ratify our own most human experiences. Let us bring ritual back into our personal lives, into our families and classrooms, into our parish festivities. For ritual, symbol, and myth is that expression which marries what is divine with what is most human in us. The making of a ceremony or a ritual is not just something that we do to or for our children. Certainly we have already had the profound experience of doing something which began as a "project to include the children," and discovered that our own involvement touched *us* deeply. The symbolic life requires us to strip down to what is basic and essential in us, and there we come upon the child within. Unless we become as little children, unless we involve ourselves just as directly as a child will who digs in the sand, who carries his Easter fire home, who blows out the candles on his birthday cake, we cannot enter into the kingdom of heaven. Ritual is the place where our humanity crosses with the transcendent. Ritual is the place where we *find* faith.

To end our considerations of the mythic, the ritual, and the symbolic life, I would like to share with you something that was introduced to me when I was in the second grade. It was given to me in a little book which I still have and still value. It was something which was not so lofty that it was over my head. It was something so real and direct that I never outgrew it. That is symbolic life at its best.

Romano Guardini, the classic liturgist, in his superb and timeless little booklet, *Sacred Signs*, which was written in 1930, gives us a meditation appropriate for a sign and ritual that we have always available to us—the Sign of the Cross. I would like to end with his short meditation. It is both so profound and so simple that it speaks to people of any age. It is the sort of meditation we can do with our children. It is the sort of thing that we can do for ourselves. This is what he says:

> You can make the Sign of the Cross, and make it rightly. Nothing in the way of a hasty waving of the hand, from which no one could understand what you are doing—no, a real sign of the cross: slow, large, from forehead to breast, and from one shoulder to the other. Don't you feel that it takes in the whole of you? Gather up all thoughts and all feelings into this sign, as it goes from forehead to breast; pull yourself together, as it goes from shoulder to shoulder. It covers the whole of you, body and soul; it gathers you up, dedicates you, sanctifies you.

> Why? Because it is the sign of the whole man and the sign of redemption. On the Cross our Lord redeemed all persons. Through the Cross he sanctifies the whole person, to the very last fibre of his being.

> That is why we cross ourselves before our prayers, so that the sign may pull us together and set us in order, may fix thoughts, heart, and will in God. After prayers we

cross ourselves, so that what God has given us may stay with us. In temptation, that it may strengthen us; in danger, that it may protect us; when a blessing is given, that the fullness of life from God may be taken into our soul, and may consecrate all in it and make it fruitful.

Think of this when you make the sign of the cross. It is the holiest sign there is. Make it carefully, slowly; make a large one, with recollection. For then it embraces your whole being, body and soul, your thoughts and your will, imagination and feeling, doing and resting; and in it all will be strengthened, stamped, consecrated in the power of Christ, in the name of the Holy Trinity. (Guardini)

(Portions of the chapter are taken from the author's *To Dance with God: Family Ritual and Community Celebration*. Mahwah, NJ: Paulist Press, 1986.)

## WORKS CITED

Guardini, Romano. *Sacred Signs*. London: Sheed and Ward, 1930.

Merton, Thomas. *The Inner Experience*. Spencer, MA: St. Joseph's Abbey.

Turnbull, Colin. *The Human Cycle*. New York: Simon and Schuster, 1983.

# 5

# ESSAY:
# LITURGY BEGINS AT HOME:
# HOUSEHOLD SACRAMENTS AND
# CHILDHOOD SPIRITUALITY

### JACK MIFFLETON

A child's first community is the family. For the small child it is the only meaningful community and source of self-identity. This means that Christian children are home-grown. When children enter school they begin to enlarge their social structures and become part of many sub-communities, but the family remains primal.

Unless children have experienced some form of religious ritual within the family (ideally in a family that is comfortable with rituals), they will be at a loss in the liturgies of the Church. Ritual readiness begins in the home, and parents are the first ritual makers.

Most children have some basic awareness of public secular rituals such as sporting events, holidays, public memorials, and the like. But what about family rituals? What in the family bears witness to the day-to-day nature of being Christian? How does a modern family search out and celebrate transcendence in its own style? The institutional sacraments themselves have their roots in family spiritual phenomena. Family faith is the basis for the community's spirituality.

The simple fact is that a child is blessed and grows in faith within a family that has Christ in its births and deaths, in its sickness and pain, in its personal traditions and family events, and in its words, touches, meals, myths, and memories. This is what fills the pages of the family faith album. These are household sacraments, the stuff of childhood spirituality. Of course, a child's experience of the family story differs from that of the adults, but it is no less real.

## THE FAMILY MEAL

The family meal is a household sacrament even though baby Billy has just poured tomato soup on his head! Our early ancestors worshipped around an open fire. Evidence suggests that they did not use the fire for cooking but ate their food raw and sat around the fire as a kind of altar. Our Judeo-Christian history brings another kind of altar into our lives—the family history. The *Directory for Masses with Children* (and such Masses are often family affairs) recommends that children first experience the human values found in the Eucharist; namely, they should experience the Eucharist as a meal of friendship (DMC 9). The larger implications are built from here. A child's search for the holy begins at the table where the family story unfolds.

## LANGUAGE

Language is a household sacrament. Often when a child, an adolescent, or even an adult complains that the language of liturgy is irrelevant or out of touch with the modern world, they might actually be admitting that they only feel comfortable with a one-dimensional language. The language of faith is multi-dimensional, like a parable or poetry. The language of story-telling and fairy tales is a means by which a child can first participate in the emotions and experiences of others. Story is an "open sesame" to a child's heart. According to Goldman, "for children fantasy is an activity which later develops into a more disciplined poetic and artistic expression of experience. Imagination is the gateway out of the concrete of literalism into the wider spiritual world" (Goldman 109). To a small child chronological time as "next year" seems distant and unreal, but a "once-upon-a-time" is close and familiar, serving as a child's introduction to sacred time and place. This language is a birthplace for faith. Healthy children speak it fluently and will share it with you for a smile and a hug.

## MEMORY

Memory, imagination, and faith come together in prayer. In liturgical prayer this is called *anamnesis*, the ability to remember with faith and imagination. Liturgists use the Greek word *anamnesis* to describe a Semitic understanding of memory which is not wholly contained in the English word "memory." This liturgical remembering is memory plus—plus faith and imagination. Liturgical memory is not the kind of memory that recalls what one had for dinner last night. It is mythic memory. For example, when a young couple meet for the first time, perhaps with dinner and a movie, and a few weeks later recall the details of that date, memory is not very deep in mythic meaning. But when they remember that first meeting after 40 years of marriage and a life together with its ups and downs, joys and sorrows, it is a different and richer remembering. Forty years of living and dying are now brought to bear on the original memory, and what it will be when this couple lie down to die and what it makes of them all their days until then, that is the real memory, that is sacramental remembering.

In 1799 in southern France a boy was found living alone in the woods. The film *Wild Child* was based on this discovery. The boy was evidently abandoned at an early age but somehow survived, living alone with the animals. When he was found at about 11 years old, he could not speak but grunted like an animal, walked on all fours and was lacking any signs of human emotional response. A physician took the child into his care and attempted to teach him some human characteristics. His success was limited. After a number of years the boy was able to speak only a few words, keep himself clean, and eat more or less properly. Little more was ever done. He had missed the vital process of socialization. He was untouched, unfamilied, and he had no power to remember imaginatively, no power of *anamnesis*. Bread and wine would have only one meaning for this boy—food. His God-like quality of wonder had atrophied.

For our children there is no spiritual survival without a familial context of one sort or another, if not of blood then of emotional bonds. A family weaves the fibers of faith and spirituality in the person building process through touching, playing, remembering, and being together. A child's spirituality follows his or her socialization process. Parents are the first ritual makers. Home is where the ability to enter into "liturgical memory" begins.

## FAMILY TRADITIONS

Family customs, traditions, myths, and memories are also places for children to meet mystery, and thus these can be seen as household sacraments. Every New Year's Day my family eats, among other things, black-eyed peas and stewed tomatoes. It is an old Virginia custom, for luck, I think. Despite the fact that I have not been at my family home for many years on New Year's Day, I can never remember celebrating the day without eating my black-eyed peas. I have even carried them with me when eating out on that day. The truth is I am not even that fond of black-eyed peas. So what is going on here? "Connectedness" is going on here. Holy ties are being renewed over thousands of miles through this ordinary mundane rite.

The pagan celebrants of northern Europe knew for many years that their yearly spring rites were not actually bringing the earth back to life and influencing the growth of plants, but nevertheless they continued the practice. We adults know there is no cause-effect relationship between blowing out candles on the birthday cake in one breath and our wish coming true, but we do it, if given the chance. If children are disposed to recognize only tangible rewards, it may be difficult to understand why people eat black-eyed peas on New Year's Day, when they dance on the green in spring, blow out candles on a cake, or break bread together, when they do not expect to get something measurable out of it.

What the childlike celebrants of family feasts receive is the basic awareness of "belonging" among other human beings, of feeling and acting in harmony. If we look around today, we see a great number of the world's youth groping for some means of belonging, of "familying" themselves. Often they go to some frightening extremes in their search. Simple family festivals can ritualize unity and affection, giving depth and preparing the family to celebrate its faith in a larger forum. These are holy rites.

# WONDER

Looking in our own story for liturgical building blocks means that our prayer is based on our ability to extract the sacred from the ordinary. The gift of a child's wonder is a household sacrament. It is upon this quality that prayer begins.

In *Pilgrim at Tinker Creek*, Annie Dillard writes that when she was about seven years old for some reason she liked to hide a precious penny of her own for someone else to find. She would place the penny at the roots of a sycamore or in a hole or crack in the sidewalk. Then she would take a piece of chalk and, starting at the end of the block, she would draw huge arrows from both directions, with signs saying "Surprise Ahead" or "Money This Way." She said the thought of a lucky passer-by finding a free gift from the universe excited her. But now she asks: "Who gets excited about a penny?" "Perhaps," she says, "it is dire poverty indeed when a person is so malnourished and fatigued that he can't stop to pick up a penny" (Dillard 14–15). A healthy simplicity and poverty can make finding a penny very life-giving, for you have brought something precious with your poverty. You have brought "wonder." It is that simple. Bright copper pennies are waiting to be uncovered by anyone with the time and imagination to look.

Prayer presumes an ability to look, to perceive what is not apparent, to find something extraordinary in the seemingly ordinary such as a penny or bread or wine. Through imagination and wonder children enter the realm of sacred time and place in order to hear a sacred language and to become sacred people.

## DEATH

A final example of a household sacrament is death. Nothing can bring a family together, at least physically, like death. When I think of a relative of blood or water, I think of a person whose death would influence my living. If Christian families find it artificial to rejoice in a life well-lived, or if they remain in their grief too long, it may mean that they view resurrection as something for the church but not for the family; that the paschal event is seen as mere religious prattle and not as a style of life.

Many of us have had the experience of telling a small child a story, and after arriving at a satisfying ending ("They all lived happily ever after."), the child looks up at you and asks: "What happened next?" or "Tell it to me again." A sequel is born. Endings always cry out for new beginnings. It is the stuff of fairy tales, and yet the signs of hope and Easter meanings are incipient in the simple question of a child.

The story of a child's faith is told through the family's births and deaths, through its words and touches, and through its traditions, meals, and memories. These are but a few household sacraments, events through which children are hallowed and grow in readiness to celebrate in the larger Christian community.

## FAMILY MASS

Within such a context the occasional Sunday family Mass brings the "domestic church"—the family—into contact with the larger faith community. These celebrations are successful when they are prepared in a way that respects and honors children, allowing them to enter the community's prayer according to their own abilities.

These specialized liturgies have limitations and depend on the larger worshipping community for intelligibility. A children's liturgy or a family Mass with a large focus on children is not in itself an adequate sign of the Church becoming church. Helping children learn the hows and whys of worship can make sense only if there exists an adult community of faith of which the children can be a part. The well-planned family Mass, however, can give children a sense of belonging and provide a consistent and steady vision and voice for life and hope against the noise that clamors to dehumanize them. Children in their own way are capable of perceiving the paschal character of liturgy and life.

## WORKS CITED

Dillard, Annie. *Pilgrim at Tinker Creek*. New York: Harper and Row, 1974.

Goldman, Ronald. *Readiness for Religion*. New York: Seabury, 1970.

Section Four

# FAMILY AND RITUAL: CELEBRATING CULTURAL TRADITIONS

# 1

# ESSAY:
# CULTURE, FAITH, AND RITUAL

*MARK R. FRANCIS, CSV*

Anyone who has wrestled with liturgy preparation knows that the word "culture" is used in many different ways. The more "culturally sensitive" in the parish often contend that for liturgy to be effective, it must incorporate customs and folk rites borrowed from the various cultures present in the parish. In doing this we somehow respond to the demands of "inculturation." But "peace and justice" people also tell us that our worship should be "counter-cultural"; it should challenge pervasive values such as "individualism" and "consumerism" present in American "culture." Youth ministers also challenge the liturgy team to adapt the worship of the parish to today's "youth culture"; this kind of challenge logically presumes that culture is a function of age. It therefore follows that we should also be sensitive to "baby-boomer culture," "middle aged culture," and "golden age culture." Finally, there is often a group of people in the parish who nostalgically yearn for the liturgical "good-old-days" and want to promote what could be described as "Catholic culture" in worship: traditional music like Gregorian chant and the solemn "smells and bells" which characterized the liturgy of their youth. Since the term "culture" is used in each of these instances in a different way, it would be helpful to discuss briefly the meaning of this term and how it relates to the worship of the Church.

## THE CHANGED UNDERSTANDING
## OF "CULTURE"

The accepted range of meaning of the word "culture" has changed radically over the last 100 years. In nineteenth century Europe and the U.S. the term connoted the great achievements of Western civilization, especially in the plastic arts, music, and literature. The paintings of Raphael, Titian, and Watteau; the music of Bach, Mozart, and Beethoven; and the literary works of Dante, Shakespeare, and Cervantes were part of that enduring legacy in the humanities which transcended national (European) borders and which constituted "culture" in the language of the educated elite. The legacy of ancient Greece and Rome—with their traditions of philosophy, law, architecture, and literature—also exercised a profound influence on the cultural achievements of generations of Europeans and Americans. One only need look at the many civic and religious buildings in any European or U.S. city built before the year 1900 to see this fascination with "classical culture." A person was considered "cultured" when exposed to and schooled in these expressions of Western civilization that educated people held up as the norm by which all other human traditions and ways of life were judged.

This rather narrow conception of culture was challenged at the beginning of the twentieth century by the emerging social sciences. Anthropology, ethnology, and sociology inspired a re-evaluation of what Bernard Lonergan described as a classicist notion of culture that regarded European culture as universal, permanent, and the model for all human achievement (Lonergan xi). These empirical sciences, which attempted to speak of human life through direct observation of human societies, increasingly spoke of human *cultures* rather than culture. Every human being, they contended, belongs to a culture which is no better or no worse than European culture. They thus relativized the conscious and unconscious claim of Europeans that their traditions represented the standard by which all other cultures should be measured. Therefore, according to the social sciences, all human beings have a "culture" and are "cultured" insofar as they share in the world view of the particular human groups in which they are born.

This changing perspective on culture also affected the self-understanding of the Church. Both Roman Catholic and Protestant missionary activity in non-Western countries was often perceived by native peoples as simply an extension of a colonial strategy to dominate non-Europeans. To become a Christian in Asia or Africa often meant to adopt European customs and to reject indigenous ways of life that were somehow inferior or simply superstitious. This identification of Christianity with European civilization was aptly summed up by Hilaire Belloc's famous phrase, "The Faith is European and Europe is the Faith" (Belloc 261).

The new movement toward a less ethnocentric understanding of culture by the social sciences also promoted the Church to review its missionary efforts and to gradually restrain itself from imposing European customs on converts who were not European. It was not until Vatican II, however, that the Roman Catholic Church would unambiguously recognize the relativity of European culture in its mission of evangelization. We will take up this revolutionary change of attitude after trying to arrive at a definition of culture.

## A WORKING DEFINITION OF CULTURE

What is culture? One of the best working definitions is offered by Clifford Geertz. Geertz defines culture as "a system of inherited conceptions expressed in symbolic forms by means of which human beings communicate, perpetuate and develop their knowledge about, and their attitudes toward life" (Geertz 89). By stating that culture is "a system of inherited conceptions," Geertz means to imply that it is something which human beings learn from their elders. Culture is not something we are "born with." It is obvious, for example, that a girl born in Australia but raised in Paris by French parents is going to speak French "like a native" and act like any other of her French peers: her heart will probably be stirred by the *Marseillaise*; she will look upon kangaroos as exceedingly exotic beasts; and she will probably go on vacation in August like the rest of the Parisians. In short, the child's vision of life will be French, not Australian. It is that vision of life, learned over the course of our childhood, that allows us to make sense out of the world in which we live; it provides meaning and order for our existence, telling us who we are and what the world is about. Family relationships, attitudes toward sexuality, styles of education, the relative position of males and females, and the laws which govern human conduct are all products of a particular world view that is formed by culture.

Although culture is learned, it is not primarily appropriated in a classroom. As Geertz notes, culture "communicates, perpetuates and develops" inherited conceptions and attitudes about the world by means of *symbolic* forms. One of the primary symbolic forms of communication is language—human speech—a way of communicating that is inextricably bound up with the particular culture that uses it. One only need think of the contemporary furor between Quebec and the rest of Canada over the preservation of French in the midst of a North American sea of English to appreciate the importance of language in expressing cultural identity. The Gaelic slogan of the nationalists in Ireland who fought for independence from Great Britain in the 1920s, *"gan teanga, gan tir"* (without language, without country) also expresses the crucial importance of language in forming national identity.

While language is a vital symbolic medium of cultural expression, it is not the only one. The fine arts such as music, dance, art, and architecture, as well as the more informal but no less important expressions of cultural values such as eating with a knife and fork, looking at the person one is addressing, and obeying traffic laws while driving a car, are just a few of the "symbolic forms" that express the values and the vision of a particular culture. All of these forms have been influenced by the history of a given people in a specific place and time. There is nothing intrinsically "better" about any of these modes of behavior—or constitutive of being human. They are particular choices selected out of a range of possible options by people who share a common view of the world. These choices both express this shared vision of reality and regulate social interaction. Aesthetic choices such as the juxtaposition of colors, dance movements, musical rhythm and tonality, as well as social conventions such as table manners, are all alternative choices people of a culture make along the course of their history and then share with future generations. There is nothing essentially "more correct," for example, about eating with a knife and fork instead of with one's hands or with chopsticks; in the Orient, looking directly at someone while talking to them can be considered aggressive and rude; and anyone who has driven in Italy knows that following traffic laws to the letter is considered aberrant behavior.

## VATICAN II AND CULTURE

Vatican II acknowledged this relativity of cultural expression in one of the final documents of the Council, the *Pastoral Constitution on the Church in the Modern World*. The entire second chapter of the document is devoted to a prolonged discussion of culture and its relationship to the Gospel. In one of the articles that begins this discussion the Council states that:

> ...culture necessarily has historical and social overtones, and the word "culture" often carries with it sociological and ethnological connotations; in this sense one can speak about a plurality of cultures. For different styles of living and different scales of values originate in different ways of using things, of working and self expression, of practicing religion and behavior, of establishing laws and judicial institutions, of developing science and the arts, and of cultivating beauty. (n. 53)

This new understanding of culture has profound implications for Christianity as a world of religion. Much of what previous generations of well-meaning Christians thought to be essential to the faith was, in reality, simply its European cultural expression. The *Pastoral Constitution* frankly admits that over the course of the centuries the Church, in order to proclaim effectively the good news of Christ, has adapted the style of this proclamation to the various cultural contexts in which it has found itself.

> Living in various circumstances during the course of time, the Church, too, has used in her preaching the discoveries of different cultures to spread and explain the message of

Christ to all nations, to probe it and more deeply understand it, and to give it better expression in liturgical celebrations in the life of the diversified community of the faithful. (n. 58)

The Council then states categorically that there is not one culturally normative way to be Christian and that the relationship between the Gospel and culture needs to be a two-way street: a dialogue which mutually enriches both those who bring the message of Christ and the "host" culture.

But at the same time, the Church, sent to all peoples of every time and place, is not bound exclusively and indissolubly to any race or nation, nor to any particular way of life or any customary pattern of living, ancient or recent. Faithful to her own tradition and at the same time conscious of her universal mission, she can enter into communion with various cultural modes, to her enrichment, and theirs too. (n. 58)

The great challenge for today's Church is to determine what is essential to the proclamation of the Christian message and what is historically and culturally conditioned, and hence changeable. This is an even more urgent challenge for those who minister liturgically with multicultural communities, since pastoral agents are often called upon not only to interpret the meaning of particular cultural expressions, but to judge whether or not these expressions accurately communicate the message of Christ.

## CULTURE AND RITUAL

It is in religious ritual that the interrelation between a particular culture and the faith of its members is most powerfully expressed. Ritual in this sense is not simply the texts and rubrical directions written down in the official books but also encompasses how the ritual is enacted and understood by the people who are engaged in worship. Their interpretation of these ritual acts is necessarily conditioned by culture: how they view the world and their place in it; the history of the relationship between the Gospel and the society from which they come; and their own experience of the divine mediated by cultural expressions.

It is often difficult to discover the relative meaning and importance of ritual gestures in another culture. Liturgy, as ritual communication, conveys meaning symbolically; and symbolic actions often speak much more forcefully than words. Liturgical symbols—whether the use of oil, incense, water, bread and wine—have power to communicate precisely because there is not simply one way to interpret them.

Respect for liturgical symbols demands that we place them in a cultural context—even if these symbols are familiar to us as part of our own cultural inheritance through the Roman Rite.

## TWO DANGERS

Thus far, we have spoken of culture as the particular world view that human beings share with others in the society in which they were raised. Such a view of the world helps individuals and societies make sense out of the chaos of human existence. The liturgy employs a broad range of symbolic actions taken from the culture in which the Church finds itself in order to express the message of Christ.

Having said all this, there are two subtle but very real dangers into which well-meaning pastoral agents can fall, especially in ministering within a multicultural community. The first is to regard the "culture" of a given group within the parish as something static and unchanging; the second is to delude oneself into thinking that Christianity can first be reduced to its "essence" and then translated into the language, signs, and symbols of a particular culture.[1]

The first danger is to so respect the different cultures within the parish as to think that the various people who are a part of them all live in a vacuum and are unaffected by the other cultures which make up the community and the larger society. There is a certain tendency among ministers sensitive to cultural issues to regard any change in existing patterns of life and worship brought about by contact with the wider community as a kind of imperialism which leads to assimilation and a tragic loss of cultural identity.[2] To a certain extent the fears of these ministers is justified and Christianity's track record in this regard is not an inspiring one. Generations of Hispanics in this country, for example, have been given the message by both the dominant culture and Church authorities to assimilate, that is to become "Americans," in order to enter into the mainstream of national life and become "worthy" of the ministrations of the Church.

There is some evidence that this insensitive and unreasonable attitude is changing on the part of the U.S. Catholic Church. However, if those who prepare the liturgy in the Hispanic community have as their goal a faithful reproduction of worship as it is done in a small Mexican village, their efforts will invariably fail to engage all but the most culturally isolated members of the community. It will fail because the people of an urban, multicultural parish in the U.S. are no longer living in a Mexican village. It will inevitably fall short of what the liturgy can achieve because the people gathered for worship lead lives which necessarily bring them into contact with people of other cultures with whom they must live and work. This contact ought to be ritually expressed because it is part of their lives. When we gather as a Christian community for worship, we gather to celebrate that action of God in Christ experienced in our lives today in whatever circumstances we find ourselves. Liturgy must celebrate the present movement of God's spirit, otherwise it degenerates into a comforting exercise in nostalgia that has nothing to do with the world in which we live.

Another equally dangerous idea is to think that all we need do in order to prepare "successful" liturgies which speak to different cultures is to arrive at the "essence" of Christianity shorn of its previous cultural associations and then simply translate this "essence" into the symbolic language of the group with whom we are ministering.

As Christians we can never preach a disembodied word of God. Rather, we proclaim that the Word became flesh in

Jesus of Nazareth who was born a Jew in the Roman province of Palestine during the turbulent period of the first century. Our faith, our experience of God, and our worship even today must be informed by the reality of the incarnation of Christ. It is also necessarily influenced by the subsequent incarnation of his body—the Church—in those cultures which embraced the Good News up to the present day. While we speak of faith in Christ as universally valid for all humanity, and "not bound exclusively and indissolubly to any race or nation, nor to any particular way of life or any customary pattern of living, ancient or recent" (*Church in the Modern World*, n. 58), this faith can only be proclaimed in an incarnated way, that is, through a particular cultural manifestation of the faith.

Those involved in pastoral ministry need to admit that their presentation of the Good News is conditioned by a particular background and by the way they see the world, and they should not delude themselves into thinking that they can somehow overcome the limitations of their own background and cultural values and preach the "essence" of the faith completely unaffected by their own cultural biases. True adaptation of both the faith and the liturgy in a multicultural community can only take place when people realize that they speak and act out of a particular cultural vision and yet are open to having this vision altered by honest dialogue with those who do not share this same vision.

It is comforting to know that the problem of proclaiming the Good News of Christ in a multicultural community is as old as the Church.

## END NOTES

[1] See the African theologian Theoneste Nkeramihigo for a discussion of these two dangers which he describes as "the danger of partitioning cultures," and "the illusion of isolating Christianity in its essence" in "Inculturation and the Specificity of the Christian Faith," *Inculturation: Its Meaning and Urgency*, Christian Leadership in Africa, Series n. 1 (Nairobi: St. Paul Publications, 1986) 67–83.

[2] "Assimilation" in this context refers to the abandonment of one's original cultural identity in order to take on the values and mores of another culture.

## WORKS CITED

Belloc, Hilaire. *Europe and the Faith*. New York: Paulist Press, 1920.

Geertz, Clifford. *The Interpretation of Cultures*. New York: Basic Books, 1973.

Lonergan, Bernard. *Method in Theology*. London: Darton, Longman and Todd, 1972.

*Pastoral Constitution of the Church in the Modern World (Gaudium et spes)*. *Vatican Council II: The Conciliar and Post Conciliar Documents*. Ed. Austin Flannery. Collegeville: The Liturgical Press, 1975.

# 2

# ESSAY:
# TOWARD AN AUTHENTIC AFRICAN AMERICAN CATHOLIC WORSHIP

### NATIONAL CONFERENCE OF CATHOLIC BISHOPS

## A. WORD AND SACRAMENT

77. First, when African American Catholics began to thirst for African American cultural expressions in Roman Catholic worship, they turned to those vestigial African traditions still found in the Protestant churches. Initially, some Catholics may have attempted to bring whole structures of African American Protestant worship into Catholic liturgy exactly as they experienced them. However, ecclesiological and credal differences as well as theological and sociological analyses suggest that most Baptist, Methodist, and Pentecostal practices simply cannot be, and nor should they be, translated into Catholic liturgy. Specifically:

> Though our liturgy is Catholic in that it is open to welcome the spiritual contributions of all peoples which are consistent with our biblical faith and our historical continuity, it is also Catholic in that everything that is done in our worship clearly serves (and does not interrupt) this ritual action of Word and sacrament which has its own rhythm and movement, all built on the directions, rites, and forms of the Roman Catholic liturgy as they are approved and promulgated. (Murray)

African American Catholics "understand the clear distinction between the Roman Catholic Church as a sacramental-eucharistic community and Christian churches of the Protestant tradition as evangelical" (Clark 20).

## B. SPIRITUALITY

78. Second, African American Catholics turned to "Black theology" for inspiration. This theology, which is concerned with the desire of the African American community to know itself and to know God in the context of African American experience, history, and culture, is as old as the first sermon preached by enslaved Africans to their brothers and sisters huddled together in some plantation swamp, and as new as the reflections of James Cone, Major Jones, J. Deotis Roberts, Cecil Cone, and others beginning in the 1960s (Lincoln). It is a theology of, about, and by African Americans. And while the formal proponents of this theology were a group of creative Protestant scholars, African American Catholic thinkers have used it as a point of departure to elaborate theological reflection that is both African American and Catholic (Wilmore and Cone). The contributions made to this theology are decidedly significant, but what they have added to the discussion on the nature of authentic African American Catholic liturgy is invaluable.

79. These theologians state that spirituality must be the starting point of a distinctively African American Catholic liturgy. It is a spirituality that is born of moments of the African American sense of "conversion." This conversion is neither "confected" nor produced in liturgy as much as it is nourished and sustained (Fleming 82).

80. The African American bishops, in their pastoral letter *What We Have Seen And Heard*, spoke eloquently of some of the qualities of an African American spirituality. They called particular attention to its contemplative, holistic, joyful, and communitarian nature.

81. African American spirituality "senses the awe of God's transcendence and the vital intimacy of His closeness" (WWHSH 8). Lifted up into God's presence, African Americans respond by surrendering and basking completely in marvelous mystery, whether in church on bended knee or at home in labor or at rest. This contemplative prayer is central and pervasive in the African American tradition.

## *HOLISTIC*

82. African American spirituality involves the whole person: intellect and emotion, spirit and body, action and contemplation, individual and community, secular and sacred.

> In keeping with our African heritage, we are not ashamed of our emotions. For us, the religious experience is an experience of the whole human being, both the feeling and the intellect, the heart as well as the head. It is a spirituality grounded in the doctrine of the Incarnation—our belief that Jesus is both divine and human. (WWHSH 8)

It is a spirituality needed in a society that produces "progressive dehumanization brought about by a technocratic society" (WWHSH 9).

## *JOYFUL*

83. African American spirituality explodes in the joy of movement, song, rhythm, feeling, color, and sensation. "This joy is a result of our conviction that 'in the time of trouble, He will lead me.' ...This joy comes from the teaching and wisdom of our mothers and fathers in the Faith" (WWHSH 9).

# COMMUNITARIAN

84. African American spirituality means community. Worship is always a celebration of community. Because in this

spirituality, "I" takes its meaning from "we"; "community means social concern for human suffering and other people's concern" (WWHSH 10).

# C. EMOTION: A WAY OF LEARNING

85. Third, the qualities of an African American spirituality suggest that this spirituality, which is deeply rooted in faith, has a strongly intuitive and emotive base. Nathan Jones, Jawanza Kunjufu, Alvin Pouissant, Na'im Akbar, and many others tell us that there are many ways of knowing and relating to the world.[1] The intellect is not the only way to experience reality. Reality may be experienced by emotion. Leopold Sedar Senghor expresses it best:

> The elan vital of Black Africans, their self-abandonment to the Other (e-motion) is, therefore, animated by reason—reason, note, that this is not the reason of "seeing" of European whites, which is more a reason of set categories into which the outside world is forced. African reason is more *logos* (word) than *ratio* (intellect). For *ratio* is compasses, square and sextant, scale and yardstick, whereas *logos* is the living Word, the most specifically human expression of the neuro-sensorial impression... The Black African *logos* in its ascent to the *Verbum* (transcendent) removes the rust from reality to bring out its primordial color, grain, texture, sound, and color. (Senghor 41)

This emotive way of knowing is not based primarily on the sense of sight as in the ocular, print-oriented culture of Europe, but on the African oral tradition, which tends to be poetic rather than literal.

86. Whereas the European way might be summarized in Descartes' "I think, therefore, I am"; the African model might be "I am, I dance the Other, I am." For,

> Africans do not make a distinction between themselves and the Object, whether it be a tree or stone, human or

beast.... They become receptive to the impression it emanates, and, like the blind, take hold of it, full of life, with no attempt to hold it in store, without killing it.... Black Africans are children of the third day of creation, pure sensory fields. (Senghor 41)

87. Father Clarence Joseph Rivers, noted African American liturgist, informs us that in this way of knowing "there is a natural tendency for interpenetration and interplay, creating a concert or orchestration in which the ear sees, the eye hears, and where one both smells and tastes color; wherein all the senses, unmuted, engage in every experience" (Rivers 45). This way of knowing does not exclude a discursive dimension. It simply states that emotion is the primary way of knowing among African peoples and their descendants. It attests that objective detachment and analytical explanations are useful, but are not the sole means of communicating faith (Rivers 49). And lastly, it asserts that peoples everywhere are not poetic or discursive, but both poetic and discursive.

## D. SOME RITUAL EMPHASES

88. Fourth and finally, this articulated African American spirituality comes to full expression in ritual activity, that activity where the Creator and creation meet; where the assembled look upon the face of God and do not die but are sustained (Fleming 19); where special attention is paid to space, time, action, language, preaching, and song.

### SPACE

89. The hush-harbors, places of conversion and wholeness, of prayer and preaching, of solace and forgiveness, of shout and dance, were the places where the enslaved went to worship. It was in these small-group spaces that they responded to the God of their forebears in praise, adoration, and reverence. It was in these places that God brought healing, meaning,

sustenance, and wholeness to them as individuals and as a group (Wimberly 198). Today, the holy ground on which the African American assembly gathers, hears God's life-giving Word, gives thanks in a sacrificial meal, and is sent back into the world must be a hush-harbor. As in former times, these hush-harbors may be anywhere, but they must reflect the assembly whose roots are both African and American, not simply African or American. For as surely as the hush-harbors of old formed the assembly, our new African American liturgical environments will shape those worshiping today. And as the worshipers are shaped, so too is the world in which they live.

90. The current hush-harbors must be "houses of the Church." They must be spaces that have "the power to anchor and map our human world and our Christian journey through it" (Fleming 70). They must be places that give full sway to the rich array of the auditory, tactile, visual, and olfactory senses (EACW 12). They must communicate relations with an African heritage and with the struggle of people today. They must be places that speak clearly to the reality that here in this sacred space is an African American, Roman Catholic people gathered for the celebration of word and sacrament. Consequently, this space must be attentive to and mindful of not only all that the African American community has to say, but also of all that the Church has to say about environment as well, especially in Chapters 5 and 6 of the *General Instruction of the Roman Missal* and the statement of the Bishops' Committee on the Liturgy, *Environment and Art in Catholic Worship*.

## TIME

91. The expressions, "We're going to have a good time" and "We're going to have church," sum up the African American's experience of sacred time. Although it is our duty and salvation always and everywhere to give thanks to God, gathering for liturgy is not simply an obligation. Gathering for liturgy is a time of glory and praise. Gathering for liturgy is

"passing time" with the Lord. It is a time to heal the "sin-sick" soul. It is a time to give the Spirit breathing room. It is a time to tell the ancient story, at dawn and at dusk, on Sunday and in every season. It is preeminently a time for the liturgical re-presentation of the paschal mystery: the dying and rising of Christ, that event of "the life of Jesus of Nazareth, who was born, lived, taught, ministered, suffered, was put to death, transcended death paradoxically and was proclaimed and exalted as the Christ...[This event] is celebrated in liturgy in such a way that its interpretation of the past event has a plenitude of meaning for the present. That past event becomes sacred time" (Braxton 74).

## ACTION

92. Holy hands lifted in prayer, bowed heads, bended knee, jumping, dancing, and shouting were all accepted movements in ancient African American worship because they were creative (i.e., created by the Spirit, who moves us to do so) (see Rom 8:15). In an African American liturgy today, this movement must still play a vital part, not merely because it is a vestige of an African heritage but because gesture is a long-standing tradition of Roman Catholic worship as well (EACW 56). Gestures reveal our inner feelings, hopes, fears, dreams, and longings for freedom. Furthermore:

> If we attend to our experience of bodily interaction with others, we discover that we become the persons we are through that interaction. We learn from the caring touch of a parent that we are valued and loved, and that incites in us the ability to value and love others in return. The attentive, engrossed look on the face of a conversation partner encourages us to share and develop the feelings and ideas within us. The forgiving hug of a friend loosens in us an unsuspected power to forgive. A hand stretched out to us in a moment of need teaches us how to rise above self-concern in dealing with others. In other words, we are called forth to become the persons we are by the deeds of others. (Fleming 126)

93. In both the Church and the African American community, there is great evidence of the power of posture in prayer.

> Prayer said standing with head and hands upraised becomes prayer of praise and self-commitment. Bended knees and bowed head plead and repent. Raised heads speak of hearts lifted to God. A handshake or an embrace offers a peace which the world cannot give. Hands folded as mirror images of each other bring an inner quiet and peace of soul. Sitting hollows out in us a la-like receptivity to receive a world in faith. (Fleming 126)

94. Crying out soars to heaven and joins in the great seraphic hymn. Waving hands proclaim a deep-down praise and thanks when mere words fail. And being slain in the spirit brings an abiding and quickening rest to a world-weary soul. One caveat:

> The liturgy of the Church has been rich in a tradition of ritual movement and gestures. These actions, subtly, yet really, contribute to an environment which can foster prayer or which can distract from prayer. When the gestures are done in common, they contribute to the unity of the worshiping assembly. Gestures which are broad and full in both a visual and tactile sense, support the entire symbolic ritual. When gestures are done by the presiding minister, they can either engage the entire assembly and bring them into even greater unity, or if done poorly, they can isolate. (EACW 56)

## LANGUAGE: PRAYER

95. African American liturgy is marked by a rich narrative quality. Words are important. And how words are used in prayer is critical.

> Prayer in the Black Tradition is the very center of the Christian life of Black people and continues to be the basis of hope. In those days when they dwelt in the dark valley of bondage hope was yet unborn. It was through prayer in which they found solace and temporary escape

from their sordid condition.... The prayers were so fervent, they seemed to ring up heaven. A significant and cogent feature of the prayers was the theological and sociological aspects. Their God was the same God of Abraham, Isaac, and Jacob; a captain who never lost a battle; a God of unrelenting love and forgiveness. Yet their prayers were always mindful of their brothers and sisters who shared some hope for freedom some day.... Today in an unsupportive society, prayer for Black people is still the "soul's sincere desire." (Bowyer 13–14)

96. The language of African American liturgy can be pro-clamatory in "witnessing" and attentive in listening; very personal without being exclusive; immanent while genuinely transcendent; exuberant and profoundly silent. it is a language that promotes the assembly's full active participation (SC 30).

## LANGUAGE: PREACHING

97. Words are also important in the art of preaching. James Weldon Johnson has described the role of preaching in African American worship this way:

The old-time Negro preacher was above all an orator, and in good measure, an actor. He knew the secret of oratory, that at bottom it is a progression of rhythmic words more than anything else. I have witnessed congregations moved to ecstasy by the rhythmic intonations. He was a master of all the modes of eloquence. He often possessed a voice that was a marvelous instrument, a voice he could modulate from a sepulchral whisper to a crashing thun-derclap. His discourse was generally kept at a high pitch of fervency, but occasionally he dropped into colloquial-isms and, less often, into humor. He preached a personal and anthropomorphic God, a sure-enough heaven and red-hot hell. His imagination was bold and unfettered. He has the power to sweep his hearers before him; and so he himself was often swept away. At such times his language was not prose but poetry. (Weldon 5)

98. Preaching frequently becomes a dialogue involving the preacher and the assembly. When the preacher delivers a sermon or makes an important point, the congregation may respond from their hearts: "Amen!"; "Yes, Lord!"; "Thank you, Jesus!" They may hum. And sometimes worshipers may simply raise their hands on high in silent gestures of praise, gratitude and affirmation. These responses are an acclamation of faith that neither demand nor expect any rubrics.

99. Because of the African American aesthetic appreciation of the vivid narrative form, the celebration of the Word of God in African American worship must be viewed as an experience of communal storytelling through which salvation history is related to the day-to-day lives of the faithful. The presiding minister is the leader of this storytelling experience. The presiding minister is a person of the "Book" (the Scriptures), whose role is to articulate the tale of the Christ event so that people can relate the salvation experience to their lives (Conwill 31–43).

100. Both preaching and praying are always in need of improvement. Those who are called to minister in the African American community must see it as their sacred trust to develop effective, spirit-filled, sound preaching and prayer. Both are a folk art. Thus, white and African American preacher-presiding ministers alike can benefit by learning more about the techniques of this African American liturgical art and regularly evaluating their ministry.

## SACRED SONG

101. The "soul" in African American liturgy calls forth a great deal of musical improvisation and creativity. It also calls forth a greater sense of spontaneity. The African American assembly is not a passive, silent, nonparticipating assembly. It participates by responding with its own interjections and acclamations, with expressions of approval and encouragement.

102. This congregational response becomes a part of the ritualized order of the celebrations. The assembly has a sense of when and how to respond in ways that would no more disrupt the liturgy than applause would interrupt a politician's speech or laughter a comedian's monologue. The deadly silence of an unresponsive assembly gives the impression that the Spirit is absent from the community's act of praise (SC 30).

103. African Americans are heirs to the West African musical aesthetic of the call-and-respond structure, extensive melodic ornamentation (e.g., slides, slurs, bends, moans, shouts, wails, and so forth), complex rhythmic structures, and the integration of song and dance (Maultsby 141–160). As a result, African American sacred song, as Thea Bowman noted, is:

*holistic*: challenging the full engagement of mind, imagination, memory, feeling, emotion, voice, and body;

*participatory*: inviting the worshiping community to join in contemplation, in celebration, and in prayer;

*real*: celebrating the immediate concrete reality of the worshiping community—grief or separation, struggle or oppression, determination or joy—bringing that reality to prayer within the community of believers.

*spirit-filled*: energetic, engrossing, intense; and

*life-giving*: refreshing, encouraging, consoling, invigorating, sustaining. (Bowman 3)

African American sacred song is also the song of the people, a people "who share and claim a common history, a common experience, a common oppression, common values, hopes, dreams, and visions" (Bowman 3).

104. African American Catholic worship may be greatly enhanced by spirituals and gospel music, both of which are representations of this aesthetic. But classical music, anthems, African Christian hymns, jazz, South American, African-Caribbean, and Haitian music may also be used where appropriate. It is not just the style of music that makes it

African American, but the African American assembly that sings it and the people whose spirits are uplifted by it.

## END NOTES

[1] Cf. Nathan Jones, *Sharing the Old, Old Story: Education Ministry in the Black Church* (Winona, MN: St. Mary's Press, 1982); Jawanza Kunjufu, *Developing Positive Self-Images and Discipline in Black Children* (Chicago: African-American Images, 1984); Alvin F. Pouissant, *Why Blacks Kill Blacks* (New York: Emerson Hall Publishers, 1972); Na'im Akbar, *Chains and Images of Psychological Slavery* (Jersey City: New Mind Productions, 1984); Reginald Lanier Jones, *Black Psychology* (New York: Harper and Row, 1972); and Alfred B. Pasteur and Ivory L. Toldson, *Roots of Soul: The Psychology of Black Expressiveness* (New York: Anchor Press, 1982)

[2] "To promote active participation, the people should be encouraged to take part by means of acclamations, responses, psalmody, antiphons, and songs, as well as by actions, gestures, and bearing. And at the proper times all should observe a reverent silence." (SC 30)

## WORKS CITED

Bishops Committee on the Liturgy, National Conference of Catholic Bishops. *Environment and Art in Catholic Worship.* Washington, DC: USCC Office of Publishing and Promotion Services, 1978.

Bowman, FSPA, Thea. "The Gift of African American Sacred Song." *Lead Me, Guide Me: The African American Catholic Hymnal.* Chicago: GIA Publications, 1987.

Bowyer, Richard O., Betty L. Hart, and Charlotte A. Meade, editors. *Prayer in the Black Tradition.* Nashville: The Upper Room, 1986.

Braxton, Edward. "Reflections from a Theological Perspective." *This Far by Faith*. Washington, DC: Liturgical Conference, 1977.

Clark, Donald. as cited in "Liturgical Expression in the Black Community." Bishop James P. Lyke, OFM. *Worship* 57.1 (January 1983): 20.

Conwill, Giles. "Black Preaching and Catholicism." *Ministry among Black Americans*. Indianapolis: Lilly Endowment, 1980.

Fleming, Austin. *Preparing for Liturgy*. Washington, DC: The Pastoral Press, 1985.

Howze, Joseph L., et al. *What We Have Seen and Heard: A Pastoral Letter on Evangelization from the Black Bishops of the United States*. Cincinnati: St. Anthony Messenger Press, 1984.

Johnson, James Weldon. *God's Trombones: Seven Negro Sermons in Verse*. New York: The Viking Press, 1969.

Lincoln, Eric. *The Black Church Since Frazier*. New York: Schocken, 1974.

Maultsby, Portia K. "The Use and Performance of Hymnody, Spirituals, and Gospels in the Black Church." *The Journal of the Interdenominational Theological Center* XIV.1–2 (Fall 1986/Spring 1987): 141–160.

Murray, SJ, J. Glenn. "The Liturgy of the Roman Rite and African American Worship." *Lead Me, Guide Me: The African American Catholic Hymnal*. Chicago: GIA Publications, 1987.

Ostdiek, OFM, Gilbert. *Catechesis for Liturgy*. Washington, DC: The Pastoral Press, 1986.

Rivers, Clarence Joseph. "The Oral African Tradition versus the Ocular Western Tradition." *This Far by Faith*. Washington, DC: The Liturgical Conference, 1977.

Second Vatican Ecumenical Conference. *Constitution on the Liturgy, Sacrosanctum Concilium* (SC). December 4, 1963.

Senghor, Leopold Sedar. "The Psychology of the African Negro." *Freeing the Spirit*, as cited in Clarence Joseph Rivers, "The Oral African Tradition versus the Ocular Western Tradition." *This Far by Faith*. Washington, DC: The Liturgical Conference, 1977.

Wilmore, Gayraud S. and James H. Cone, editors. *Black Theology: A Documented History*. Maryknoll: Orbis Books, 1979.

Wimberly, Edward. "The Dynamics of Black Worship: A Psychological Exploration of the Impulses that Lie at the Roots of Black Worship." *The Journal of the Interdenominational Theological Center* XIV.1–2 (Fall 1986/Spring 1987): 198.

# 3

# GUIDELINES FOR CULTURAL SENSITIVITY: AFRICAN AMERICANS

*EVA MARIE LUMAS, SSS*

Any serious discussion of African American families must be prefaced with four considerations: 1) The current crisis of the African American family is indicative of the social, political, economic and ethical crisis that pervades all of contemporary American life. African American families are thus in the process of reorganizing themselves to find effective ways of dealing with the larger societal situation in which they live. 2) Much more research on African American families remains to be done regarding cultural traits, organizational structures, functional roles of family members and interactive patterns. 3) The "average" African American has not studied the research that does exist. Much of their family cultural norms, organizational structures, functional roles, etc. are done instinctually or consequent to unspoken directives within the culture. 4) The diverse approaches utilized to study African American families requires those who attempt to address African American family life to cite their sources so that their bias can be readily identified. Apropos to this, I have attached a bibliography at the end of these guidelines to indicate the research and theories that have influenced my thinking.

1.  The principal functions of the African American family are to provide subsistence (care for physical needs), nurturing, guidance, support, protection, and mobility for its members. In addition, the African American family teaches its members how to overcome the handicap of their inferior social status, the lack of equitable access to resources within society at

large, and the general hostilities of personal and institutional racism.

Therefore, ministers should be sensitive to the general and the specific functions of African American families. And they should develop policies, programs and strategies in collaboration with blacks that support and enhance the principle functions of African American families by influencing public policy and developing other means of helping African Americans to achieve equality in the areas of economic development, education, employment, housing, health care, and legal representation.

2.  The organizational structure of African American families serves the functional needs (psychological, social, emotional, cultural, and spiritual) of black people.

   a. Black family life is not a deviant expression of white family life.

   b. The organizational structure, functional roles, interactive patterns and values of African American families reflect the nature and circumstance of being black in America.

   c. Some characteristics of African American families are carry-overs from Africa; some are adaptations of family life within America's dominant culture. And some characteristics are adaptations of African family life which offer alternatives to the family life of America's dominant culture. The following examples illustrate the point:

      1. African carry-over: When an older black person resides in the home of one of their children the elder person is usually regarded as the head of the household.

      2. Adaptation of family life in the dominant culture: Blacks do not perceive a single-parent family as a "broken" family. As long as the adult who is present in the nuclear family home, and the extended

family network, can provide the necessary care and nurturing required, the single-parent family is considered to be whole (healthy).

3.  Alternative to family life of dominant culture: The well-being of the extended family network has primacy over the nuclear family to which a person belongs.

Therefore, ministers need to be sensitive to the fact that African American families must be understood within the context of their own values, conceptual framework, and organizational structures. And ministers need to develop policies, programs, and strategies that enable African Americans to name and better appreciate their family experience.

3.  African American family structures, operational functions, interactive patterns and values carry the influence of its African roots. It is not simply a construct of American slavery.

a.  African Americans did not come from slavery; they came *through* slavery, steeped in the values and traditions of Africa.

b.  Contemporary research on African American families reveals that slavery did not completely destroy the cultural legacy of Africa.

c.  The following examples illustrate the inherent influence of Africa within African American families:

1.  Extended family networks resemble African tribal kinship networks.
2.  The ability of African Americans to utilize flexible gender roles is consistent with the African value of cooperative work and responsibility.
3.  High esteem given to elders.
4.  Naming children after a favored or deceased member of the family resonates with the African notion that a person lives as long as their name is remembered.

5. Shared responsibility for the extended family is consistent with the African value of cooperative sharing of resources.

6. Children are regarded as the family's greatest wealth.

7. A "broken family" is a term that refers to a breach within the extended family network, not to absence of one of the spouses in a nuclear family unit.

8. A "poor family" refers to the inability of an extended or nuclear family to provide for the basic physical, social, psychological, and spiritual well-being of its members. It is believed that once these needs are met, the rest (i.e., higher education, economic stability, etc.), will come in its own time.

9. While husbands in most African societies commonly had authority over their wives, women had considerable control over what they earned from their own labor.

Therefore, ministers need to remember that even though some of the behavioral characteristics of African Americans appear to be consistent with the behavioral norms of other ethnic and cultural groups, no simple assumptions can be made about the origin or meaning of behavior. The meaning and expected outcomes of the African American family structures, operational functions, interactive patterns, and values are rooted in an African psyche and African Americans must be allowed to describe and define their own experience.

4. The traditional strengths[1] of African American families:

a. Strong kinship bonds: African Americans are highly relational. They tend to relate to a greater number of their relatives on a regular basis than do other ethnic,

---

[1] Items "a" through "e" are contained in the research of Robert Hill; "f" through "h" are contained in the research of Wade W. Nobles; "j" is contained in the research of Niara Sudarkasa; and "k" is expressed within studies of every researcher studied.

cultural groups. Strong kinship bonds affords an individual family member considerably more resourcefulness than he or she would otherwise have.

b. Strong work ethics: The disenfranchisement of African Americans from the resources and benefits of the larger society has reinforced their need to be self-generating and self-reliant.

c. Adaptability of family roles: African Americans generally share the same gender-role definitions as the dominant culture; however, they expect family members of both sexes to participate in role performance to the extent that they are able.

d. Strong achievement orientation: African Americans share the human need for productivity, recognition, and personal-efficacy to control the details of one's life. In addition to this, however, the African American's orientation to achievement includes the need to provide for their own people those resources and services that they cannot receive from the larger society.

e. Strong religious orientation: African American people have found tremendous strength and courage from their belief in a supreme being who knows their hardship, affirms the righteousness of their efforts toward justice, and is actively engaged in opposing the forces of their oppression. Black families have taught their members that there are no permanent constraints to their ability to achieve their just ambitions as long as they are true to the will of God.

f. Legitimizing the personhood of its members: Familial relationships have nurtured positive self-images and senses of self-worth in the family's members to counteract the effects of their being treated as objects or commodities within the institutional and social structures of American life.

g. Provision of a family code: The family provides its members with guidelines and values that govern their ability to interpret and manage familiar and unfamiliar situations and relationships.

h. Provision of information and knowledge: The insights gained from family members' experiences are shared so that each member of the family has the benefit of the groups' resourcefulness in managing the events of their lives.

i. Concrete mediation of the existential circumstances and conditions of its members: Besides buffering the individual stresses of family members, this function provides group collaboration for problem solving and the assurance of recognition for achievements. In addition, this feature of the family provides collaborative decisions regarding the distribution of the family's resources.

j. Determination of interpersonal interaction: Interaction within the family is governed by the principles of mutual respect, responsibility, reciprocity, and individual restraint (Restraint may take the form of self-sacrifice for the benefit of another).

k. Provision of social-psychological safety: The family serves as a sanctuary that counteracts the ill-effects of racism and social hostilities.

Therefore, ministers need to develop policies, programs, and strategies that affirm the strengths of African American families and the role that these family strengths have had in the survival and success of blacks within American society. At the same time, ministers need to develop policies, programs, and strategies that address the ills of African American families with the purpose of reinstating the historic health, goodness, wholeness, and holiness of black family life.

5.    The special characteristics[2] of African American families:

a. Comprised of the residents of multiple households who are primarily related by blood.

b. Elastic in the sense that they may include persons and households who are not related by blood, but who share the same hopes, struggles, pains, etc. Persons who are considered to be family although they are not related by blood are often given familial titles, e.g., uncle, aunt, sister, brother.

c. Child-centered system rather than systems based on the conjugal relationship between spouses.

d. Composed of close networks of relationships between families. Blacks may regard their aunts and uncles with the same esteem as they do their parents. And blacks may regard their cousins with the same regard as they have for their siblings.

e. Able to maintain flexible and interchangeable role definitions and performance.

1.  The roles of nurturing and providing for the family have not been traditionally linked to the male or the female, but to the person who could best perform the needed function.

2.  The concept of mutual responsibility for caring for the needs of the family, mitigated against rigid adherence to traditionally defined gender boundaries.

f. Multiple parents and inter-familial consensual adaptations.

1.  The extended family network may sometimes operate in a manner that makes the eldest member

---

[2] These characteristics are contained in the research of Wade W. Nobles.

of the family (whether male or female) the head of a number of households.

2. The care and supportive functions of a family may be provided by multiple households who share the responsibility for providing for the entire family network.

Therefore, ministers need to be aware of ways that their own family experience biases their understanding of "the family" and avoid trying to understand or describe black families by comparing them to families of other ethnic, cultural groups. Ministers also need to develop policies, programs, and strategies that encourage intergenerational interaction, extended family participation, and flexible gender performance.

6.   There are many characteristics common to African Americans as a group. However, the African American community is not monolithic and African American family life is influenced by a variety of factors:

   a.   Each African American family carries the influence of its geographic origin:

   1.   Rural United States
   2.   Urban United States
   3.   Northern United States
   4.   Southern United States
   5.   Eastern United States
   6.   Western United States
   7.   Georgia Sea Islands
   8.   South Carolina Sea Islands
   9.   Caribbean Islands
   10.  Central American
   11.  South American

   b.   Each African American family carries the influence of its socioeconomic class, i.e., lower, middle or upper class.

   1.   These socioeconomic class distinctions are often poor indicators of a person's esteem within a family.

For example, persons who live at a low socioeconomic level may be regarded with high esteem due to their wisdom or insightfulness. On the other hand, persons who have risen to the upper class may be regarded with contempt because of their lack of generosity or their criticalness of other less fortunate family members (Dodson).

2. These varying socioeconomic classes will often affect how black persons view their social status; their awareness of black oppression, and their interpretation of its consequences; the degree to which they aspire to assimilate within the mainstream of American life; and the degree to which they personally identify with the black struggle for liberation.

c. Each African American family carries the influence of its educational level.

1. While African Americans have historically believed that education is a necessary means of achieving freedom and equality, formal education is not regarded as the full measure of a person's intelligence or worth, and it is not the fulcrum of a person's achievement.

2. A high level of formal education does not automatically award a person high esteem within a family. People who forget or reject the folk wisdom of their people are regarded as "educated fools."

3. Highly educated persons who do not use their learning or the benefits it generates for the good of their people are believed to have exploited or sold their people out.

Therefore, ministers need to be conscious of the characteristics that are common to all African American families and attentive to the uniqueness of each African American family. Ministers must avoid stereotypical or generalized concepts of African Americans. At the same time, ministers need to facilitate opportunities for African Americans to tell their own story and the meaning they have ascribed to that story.

7. The extended family network of African American families are based on consanquineal (blood relationships) rather than conjugal bonding patterns.

   a. The extended family serves to buffer the effects of unmet needs in the nuclear family. In addition, the extended family expands and reinforces the effective resources of the nuclear family.

   b. Blacks regard their extended family to be primarily, but not exclusively, comprised of those persons who are related by blood.

   c. The spouses and children of blood relatives are incorporated into the extended family to the extent that these persons comply with the foundational principles and general priorities of the group.

   d. Divorce does not necessarily sever the extended family's tie to the spouse of a blood relative as the family may empathize with the spouse.

   e. The children and/or "step-children" of blood relatives are not excluded from the extended family due to the divorce of their parents. They are still regarded as "the family's children."

Therefore, ministers need to develop policies, programs, and strategies that reinforce the "corporate identity" of African Americans. When African Americans gather as a faith community during times of tragedy or celebration, ministers should address the family's need to strengthen its bonds and heal its divisions. During the normal course of the family's participation in the church, ministers should find ways to involve whole families into church ministries, programs and events.

8. African American families are person-centered, yet community-oriented.

a. The family network can make allowances for the individual styles, personalities, contributions, conditions and/or circumstances of its members.

b. The idiosyncratic and novel aspects of individual personalities are generally encouraged and appreciated, especially when they add to the general well-being of the group.

c. The family expects individual members to occasionally compromise their personal preferences and/or styles for the good of the group.

d. An individual's personal identity is strongly rooted in his or her corporate identity as a member of the family.

Therefore, ministers need to remember that African Americans are often caught in a dilemma in the church: blacks are frequently, rather than occasionally, expected to compromise their perspectives or desires for the "good of the larger church community." Ministers who are generally not willing to value the black person or black people over the norms, traditions, or rules that benefit others will quickly lose their credibility with blacks. The uncompromising attitudes of these ministers will result in their being labelled as an uncaring attitude. Policies, programs, and strategies need to be developed that encourage African Americans to contribute their insight, style, talent, preferences, and personalities to the church.

9. African American families suffer immense pressure from black male-female conflict due to displaced anger resulting from institutional racism and an attempt to adopt the gender role definitions of the dominant culture.

a. African Americans generally embrace the traditional American ideologies of male-female roles within the family. However, black men and black women are not provided with the means of implementing their ideals.

1. Most black men are excluded from the social-economic systems that maintain America's notion

of "manhood." As a result they cannot perform the traditionally prescribed masculine family roles.

2.  Unable to find a sufficient number of black men who have attained the prescribed notions of "manhood", most black women who marry will assume masculine family roles (i.e., they become the provider) or they give up on the attempt to marry at all.

b.  Saddled with unrealistic expectations of each other, black men and black women are primed for conflict with each other.

1.  The alleged "black matriarchy" is the invention of those who choose to blame black women for the continued decimation of black men in American society. However, black women do not control the legal system, social structures, economy, schools, or propaganda networks that debilitate black men.

2.  The propagation of black male stereotypes that depict them as socially violent, domestically indifferent, interpersonally callous and socio-economically inept, acts as a self-fulfilling prophesy that erodes their self-esteem and undercuts their relationships.

c.  The high incidence of female-headed households are the direct consequence of America's institutional structures: There is a direct relationship in the level of black male unemployment and number of black female-headed households.

d.  The particular circumstances of being black in America have placed African American women in positions that are socially prescribed for men:

1.  Social institutional structures put large numbers of black women into the work-force, even though most of their jobs were once domestic. As early as 1900 almost half of all black women in America were in the labor force. At the same time, black men were

barred from the economic means necessary to assume the socially prescribed masculine role as the family's provider.

2. The socialization process of black women teaches them to aspire for traditionally prescribed male-female relationships. At the same time, it also prepares them for self-sufficiency and independence due to the precarious conditions of black men.

3. Black culture's approbation of adaptability in family roles has engaged African American women in endeavors that are generally regarded as the domain of men. For example, black women have conducted family business that is external to domestic chores or the running of their household.

e. The particular circumstances of being black in America have systematically and consistently suppressed the potential of black men:

1. The educational system has left approximately 50% of the black male population ill-equipped to function successfully in a technological society.

2. Only half of all black men are in the labor force.

3. A disproportionately high number of black men are incarcerated.

4. Many black men have incomes significantly lower than their wives.

5. Negative social-psychological images of black men comprise the bulk of media attention given to them. It is ironic that Bill Cosby's portrayal of Dr. Cliff Huxtable is renounced as an incredible role model for black men, while Redd Foxx's depiction of Fred Sanford is received without criticism.

f. Negative, distorted representations of the African American family (e.g., the Moynihan Report) are more widely publicized within the black community and within American society at large, than are positive, self-reflective research of black social scientists. This must be understood as a deliberate institutional attempt to corroborate the bias of the destructive forces that continue to assault African American family life.

Therefore, ministers need to develop policies, programs, and strategies that encourage African American men and women to examine and reclaim the strengths of traditional black male-female relationships which enabled them to build stable conjugal relationships. Such an endeavor would unleash the potential for black men and black women to develop relationships characterized by self-sufficiency and networking, assertiveness and negotiation, mutual responsibility and empathy, nurturance and support.

10. The values and expectations regarding parents and parent-child relationships in African American families generally focus on providing children with 1) the skills necessary to survive in a hostile society, and, 2) the hope of succeeding in the society in spite of the hostilities.

    a. Black children have a dual socialization process that teaches them the ways of the black community and the realities of a white-dominated society.

    b. In deciding how to have a task completed, most black families will not consider a child's gender. If a child of either sex has the competence to perform a task, the child is expected to do so. Apropos to this, an older child of either sex is expected to care for the younger children in his or her family.

    c. Most black families do not use psychological methods to discipline a child, such as making a parent's affection conditional to the child's performance. Black families are generally very direct and physical in the correction of a child.

    d. Black families of all socioeconomic levels attempt to reinforce similar positive values in their children: personal values (i.e., generosity, fairness), racial-cultural pride, sound morals, self-control, and the need for an education.

e. Black families of all socioeconomic levels suffer race-related stress in the rearing of their children:

1. They must teach their children how to effectively participate in the black community so that they will not be displaced within the society. And they must teach their children how to effectively participate in the white community so that they will not be disenfranchised from the society.

2. Because of their general feeling of vulnerability, they will often choose not to directly or publicly confront a racially-motivated affront to a child unless the effects on the child are extreme.

   i. The family may simply tell the child to ignore the incident.

   ii. The family may over-simplify the incident with explanations or excuses.

   iii. The family may distort the incident to camouflage the racial intent.

   In any of these scenarios, the child learns not to look to his or her family for protection. The child learns to doubt his or her right to be protected. And the child may learn to deny or distort the reality and ill-effects of racial assault.

f. African American children who are taught to identify and confront racial incidents develop more healthy self-concepts, self-confidence, and group identity.

g. Black men and black women share the responsibilities of decision making and care for their children.

h. Black parents expect emotional support from black grandparents and other members of their extended families for the rearing of children.

i. Child-rearing within single-parent homes is strained when extended family networks break down or when the parenting is being done by a teenager.

j. African American families of all socioeconomic levels experience stress in child-rearing due to their children's exposure to and adoption of the prevailing negative values of the society, i.e., individualism, self-determined decision-making regarding the use of money, early sexual activity, and the prominence of substance abuse.

k. Most black parents regard religion to be a primary resource for child-rearing.

l. The participation of African American youth in the church is strained:

1. Black youth often do not perceive the church's understanding of the realities of their lives.
2. Black youth often do not perceive the church's youth ministry programs to be equivalent options to the events and relationships that engage them within the larger society.
3. Black youth often do not perceive the church to have a critical or credible impact in the quality of their lives or their future.

Therefore, ministers should develop policies, programs, and strategies that foster healthy parent-child relationships, alleviate part of the stresses of child-rearing, address the social ills that undermine positive family (and human) values, and establish meaningful ways to manifest the church's investment in the life of black people, adults, children and youth.

11. Integration has contributed to the erosion of traditional African American family structures, functions, and stability.

a. The relatively high geographic mobility of African Americans within American society has caused blacks to experience a new diaspora (scattering of peoples).

1. Upwardly mobile blacks are often isolated within predominantly white residential areas, schools, and places of employment.

2. Those blacks who are "left behind" in the old neighborhoods do not have sufficient access to positive black role models or to the resources gained by the successes of some of their family members.

b. African Americans who have had high levels of exposure to and interaction with whites in the last 25 years are constantly reminded that they know more about whites than whites know about them.

1. Those black people who have high levels of exposure to and interaction with whites in residential communities, schools, and places of employment have often tried to manage these situations by cultural assimilation (rejecting their own culture). In other instances these blacks are assaulted by cultural accommodation (being tolerated, but not understood or appreciated by the dominant culture).

2. Many black children who attend integrated schools have learned to cope with their inferior status by attempting to assimilate with their white peers. The developmental need of youth for peer approval coupled with the isolation of these youth from their extended family with its history, values, norms and world-view, makes these black youth particularly susceptible to cultural confusion.

c. The Civil Rights Movement of the 1960s sought to give African Americans greater access to the resources of American society and a more equitable share of its benefits. But the resistance of the dominant culture to relinquish its privileged status has resulted in limited achievements on the part of blacks:

1. Social class stratification is more pronounced among blacks than ever before.

2. The majority of America's black population is no better off.

3. The educational system continues to under-educate and mis-educate African Americans.

4. Social services are still inadequate and when these services are accessible, African Americans are still treated with condescension.

5. The political and legal systems continue to ignore the enduring devastations of institutional racism. Isolated, individual experiences of racial justice and cultural pluralism are cited as sufficient reason not to address racism as an institutionalized aspect of American life.

6. Religious institutions spend more time discussing the basic human similarities between blacks and whites rather than developing an appreciation for their respective cultural differences. But a people's similarities is not the source of their conflict. And more than that, the need to reduce people to their lowest common denominator is itself a means of domination and control.

Therefore, ministers need to develop policies, programs, and strategies that encourage African Americans to maintain and share the Afro-centric strengths, values, traditions, and insights inherent in their cultural heritage as a resource created by God for the benefit of the whole society.

12. The two most powerful and life-giving institutions in the life of African Americans have historically been the family and the Church.

a. The basic values of African American family life were recognized, clarified, sanctioned, and reinforced within a Christian framework through the church.

b. Historically, the church functioned as an extended family that provided spiritual, emotional, educational, social, economic, and political support to African Americans.

c. Along with the supportive programs that all Christian churches provided to their predominantly black congregations, the black church was also the storehouse of culture for African Americans.

1. Within the black church African American culture was respected and normative for its members.
2. Within the black church African American culture and spirituality united to address the realities of black life.

d. Historically, the black church enabled African Americans to develop resources (i.e., leadership skills, monetary resources, clarity of purpose, etc.) and strategies to combat racism and facilitate the ability of African Americans to move into the mainstream of American life.

e. African American Catholics have not experienced their church's direct involvement in the black community's effort to combat racism.

1. African American Catholics have historically believed that the Catholic Church's educational programs have assisted them in overcoming some of the effects of racial oppression.
2. African American Catholics have relied on the spiritual resources of their church for the inspiration to persevere in their struggle they have persistently requested the church to aid them with other concrete systematic approaches to combat oppression.

f. African American Catholics have begun to appreciate the relationship between culture and faith (including spirituality, theology, liturgy, etc.).

g. Both Protestant and Catholic African Americans now have a growing concern for their church to apply its institutional resources to combat the persistent problem of racism within the church and the society at large. Fueling this concern are the beliefs that:

1. Racism contradicts the Christian faith as it is a denial of the inherent human dignity, worth, and rights of every person.
2. The Christian church's inactivity regarding racism is believed to be an implicit and explicit communication of the church's consent or at least its indifference.

Therefore, ministers must develop policies, programs, and strategies that explicitly declare the church's opposition to racism and any forms of oppression; embrace black culture and the black experience; and further the black community's noble ambition for justice within the church and society.

## BIBLIOGRAPHY

Bowman, Sr. Thea (ed). *Families: Black and Catholic, Catholic and Black.* Washington, DC: United States Catholic Conference, 1985.

Cheatham, Harold E. and James B. Stewart. *Black Families.* New Brunswick, NJ: Transaction Publishers, 1990.

Lyke, Most Reverend James P. *The Family in the Black Community.* Cleveland: Catholic Diocese of Cleveland, OH, 1986.

Martin, Elmer P. and Joanne Mitchell Martin. *The Black Extended Family.* Chicago: University of Chicago Press, 1978.

Mathis, Arthur. "Contrasting Approaches to the Study of Black Families", Nobles, Wade W. "Toward an Empirical and Theoretical Framework for Defining Black Families", McAdoo, Harriette Pipes. "Factors Related to Stability in Upwardly Mobile Black Families" in *Journal of Marriage and the Family* (Special Issue: Black Families). November, 1978. Vol 40, No. 4.

McAdoo, Harriette Pipes (ed). *Black Families*. Beverly Hills: Sage Publications, Inc., 1981.

Roberts, J. Deotis. *Roots of a Black Future: Family and Church*. Philadelphia: Westminster Press, 1980.

Smith, Wallace Charles. *The Church in the Life of the Black Family*. Valley Forge: Judson Press, 1985.

Staples, Robert (ed). *The Black Family* (Third Edition). Belmont, CA: Wadsworth Publishing Co. Inc., 1986.

*What We Have Seen and Heard: A Pastoral Letter on Evangelization*, from the Black Bishops of the United States. St. Anthony's Messenger Press, 1984.

# 4

# ESSAY: CHARACTERISTICS OF HISPANIC WORSHIP

## *ARTURO PEREZ*

*El padrino* awoke a little earlier than usual that Saturday morning. Today was the day. As he lay there, his mind wandered back to the dinner invitation which he had received several months earlier from José and María. He had wondered why they were so insistent on meeting for dinner, and so excited when the evening arrived. In the course of the meal the reason soon became clear. "When the baby is born, we want you to be *el padrino* and our *compadre.*" It was not so much a request as an expectation stemming from the long friendship which the three had shared. "But this is your first! Shouldn't some member of your family be asked?" "No," they insisted, "this is what both of us want!" Thus ended the discussion. And the morning had finally arrived. Today the baby would be baptized.

This would be an all day event. Relatives, traveling from as far away as California, had been arriving for the day. The baptism was planned for 11:00 a.m., but that was just the beginning. Food still had to be cooked and prepared by the various friends and neighbors who had volunteered to help. Everyone would be expected to help decorate the hall. María had given *el padrino* special assignments, which included picking up the cake and the special meats from the neighborhood bakery. "Time to get moving," *el padrino* thought as he rolled out of bed.

Hispanic worship celebrates life and is centered around the sacraments. From the perspective of popular religiosity, these sacramental events help to focus on the true meaning of the life being celebrated. The four main sacramental events in the life of the Hispanic community are baptism, first Eucharist, marriage, and that complex of rituals which accompany the death of an individual, sometimes referred to as "the sacrament of death and rising."

As for the other sacraments, confirmation is celebrated by many Hispanic families when the child is still very young—perhaps only two or three years old—and is not a major moment for celebration. This practice, however, is certainly changing as parents confront the practice in the United States of confirming teenagers. Penance still remains a private moment and is usually experienced as a preparatory step for receiving some other sacrament. Holy orders—due, in part, to the lack of Hispanic role models—still has not touched most of our families, though seeds of change are being sown here with each new wave of Hispanic permanent deacon ordinations and the increase of Hispanic vocational efforts.

It may be the baptismal story just related, however, which is the more typical experience in today's Hispanic community. Furthermore, such a story well demonstrates key characteristics of Hispanic worship. Though there are various ways in which these characteristics could be enumerated, it is possible to consider them under the six following headings.

Hispanic worship is *familial*. As illustrated by our baptismal story, worship is a time for the immediate and extended family of *compadres* to gather. On special occasions like baptisms or weddings, the inconvenience and expense of travel are secondary to the gatherings of the family. It is not only on these special occasions that the family gathers for worship in the Hispanic community, however, for Sunday worship is a time for such gathering as well. Each Sunday of the year the church is transformed by the gathering community which takes possession of the building. The noise level noticeably increases as *saludos* and *abrazos* are exchanged between *compadres*, old friends, and new arrivals. Children make the aisles of the church their home as they look for ways to be entertained and cared for. Grandparents teach their grandchildren how the sign of the cross is made, how hands are to be folded and prayers are to be said. This is family as the first school of faith and the cornerstone of Hispanic worship.

Hispanic worship presumes a central role for *women*. It is especially the women of the community who are the traditional transmitters of faith through their example, their teaching, and their devotion. Further influenced by the lay leadership and feminist movements in the United States, Hispanic women are becoming even more visible in ministerial leadership. Where previously they were catechists, they are now directors of religious education; where previously they were sacristans, they are now lectors and ministers of communion; where previously they were helpful neighbors, they are now ministers to the sick and shut-ins. Hispanic women are the ones who know "the right ways" of praying for the dead, for celebrating *posadas*, and for organizing feast days. They are the new found pastoral associates, leaders of liturgy teams, and directors of social ministry. And it is their link with tradition and vision for the future which is enabling new ways of faith to grow from the old ways.

Hispanic worship is the worship of the *young*. Sociologically, Hispanics are one of the youngest ethnic groups in the United States today. In a recent background report prepared for Pope John Paul II's 1987 visit to the United States, it was reported that the median age of the non-Hispanic population in the United States is 31.9 years, whereas the median age of Hispanics is 25.1 years. Attending to the youth element in our communities, however, does not necessarily mean resorting to teen or adolescent focused worship. Rather, we need to recognize the large number of parents who become grandparents by age 40, and great grandparents by age 60. These relatively young and vital people become the "wise ones" in the parish and have the responsibility for nurturing the young generations in ways of our faith. For this they are revered and held in esteem by our community. As for the large numbers of children, adolescents, and young adults in our communities, their energy and enthusiasm is always a great promise and challenge to our worship. Conscious efforts must be made to invite them into full, conscious, and active participation in our worship and in the whole life of the church. Pastorally this suggests that our worship should be attractive and contemporary without being faddish or contrived.

Hispanic worship is characterized by a strong devotion to *Mary*. Though she has different titles in different countries, is often depicted in the dress of various regions and nationalities, and is honored by innumerable feasts and special days of devotion, she is yet for us the same woman. Mary is so identifiable because her life is so close to our own. She is poor, giving birth to a son in a stable. She is worried and anxious when the child is lost on a journey. She is the companion and follower of Jesus during his public ministry. She is the widow and grieving mother in need of consolation and comfort. She is the faithful woman who prays constantly. As with all the saints, but more than any other, she is our neighbor and friend: attentive to our worries and frustrations, supportive with her gentility and care, opening her hands and heart to us in prayer.

Hispanic worship is *musical*. Since music pervades all of life's experiences in the Hispanic community, it is natural that in our worship as well, music should serve to weave our prayer together into a unified song of praise. Among our ancestors, music was a vehicle for expressing truth. Musical liturgy is for us a proclamation of Gospel truth in rhythm, melody, and text which brings the community to life. Though this phenomenon is universal in all of the Hispanic churches, the music experience of the United States is quite different from that of the Latin or Caribbean countries. Here the guitar and percussion instruments have come to dominate, and there has been a definitive movement away from the dominance of the organ in our worship. Furthermore, in the United States more than anywhere else, melodies reminiscent of home feasts now resound through our churches. Hispanic people want to sing and willingly respond to the kind of musical leadership that invites them into the celebration.

Hispanic worship is an *embodied* experience. Life is lived in close quarters in our neighborhoods and in our homes.

Houses pushed up against each other, apartment buildings overflowing with residents, and several families sharing cramped living quarters are not unusual experiences for us. Worship like life, therefore, means rubbing shoulders with each other just like at home. This means not only being touched at home and at prayer, but it also means being physically present to each other. It means an *abrazo* rather than a handshake, taking care of everyone's children in the church as if they were your own, and being in full contact with the symbols of life so that food, drinking, washing, and anointing are all savored to their fullness and felt more than just seen. It means that our celebrations are filled with flowers and candles, colors and incense, movement and texture and light. It means the close proximity of ministers to community and community to community. It means, therefore, the ability to be touched and the freedom to touch another human being in the presence of the holy.

All of these characteristics point to one simple fact about Hispanic liturgical life: Hispanic worship is people centered rather than ritual centered. It is the gathering of the community in song and celebration more than the proper execution of the rubrics which is at the center of our public prayer. Liturgy is for us not the proper reading of a book but a movement of the community's heart, seeking to express itself in one voice and in one living prayer.

## THE INTEGRATION OF HISPANIC RITUALS AND THE ROMAN LITURGY— SELECT EXAMPLES

"You start where the people are at," said the old priest to his newly ordained associate. "You should know that by now," he gently chided. The ministerial newcomer was truly embarrassed that his youthful enthusiasm had been so blind. He had only wanted to update the first communion Mass when he suggested eliminating the extra *padrinos*, candles, and arm bands which only complicated the liturgy. In doing so, however, he had walked over the land mines of people's feelings, transforming a rather tranquil get-together into a last minute showdown between himself, parents, and members of the pastoral staff. "You start where the people are at" would be engrained in his memory forever. The old man, in turn, smiled to himself remembering *his* first experience with the "golden rule," as he hurried to answer the phone.

Beginning where people are, and not where we want them to be, is an important "commandment" for any pastoral practitioner and an essential part of the evangelization process. More than a rule, however, such an awareness translates into a style of ministry that first seeks to experience the way people live. Where prayer is concerned, it means beginning with waiting, watching, and living the experiences of another's prayer. In so doing, the minister's own prayer becomes a source of reflection: past experiences of communal and individual prayer, as well as invitations to pray in new ways, can be more deeply appreciated. Eventually ministerial leadership, communal expression, and personal appreciation converge, giving rise to prayer forms which are enriched because of such convergence.

The genius of the Roman Rite is traditionally expressed in terms of its simplicity, clarity, and brevity. These characteristics were especially apparent when the rite was celebrated exactly the same all over the world. Since the *Constitution on the Sacred Liturgy*, however, has called us not only to adapt a few externals of the rite, but to strive to truly inculturate the worship into the various cultures of the world, we may have to rethink the nature of this rite's genius. Perhaps at the present time the Roman liturgy is best understood as a kind of skeleton which is recognizable as a human being, but an unnamed human being without a specific identity. It is not until it takes on the flesh and blood of a living culture that this rite comes to life and effectively calls us to life in Christ.

For this skeleton to be enfleshed by Hispanic culture means, therefore, celebrating in Spanish, but it also means much more than just an act of translation. Though it is undeniable that language is one of the most important expressions and vehicles of a culture, it is also clear that language is only one such element. Spanish alone, therefore, cannot transform a generic, all-purpose celebration into Hispanic worship. It is, instead, only by drawing upon the full repertoire of religious and cultural symbols—which means integrating the rituals of popular religiosity with official forms of worship—that true Hispanic worship will emerge. It is such an integration which we hope to represent here with a few select examples.

## POSADAS

The *posada* is a Christmas custom of the Mexican and Mexican-American communities which re-enacts Joseph and Mary's search for an inn (*posada*) before the birth of Jesus. This ritual re-enactment traditionally occurs outdoors as a part of novena which serves as a preparation for Christmas. The *posada* specifically consists of special hymns which are sung in dialogue between two groups of people: one outside representing Joseph and Mary, and another group inside representing the innkeepers. Lodging is denied to the pilgrims several times until, at last, they are joyfully invited into the home. Once inside, the assembled community prays a Rosary and a litany, and then more hymns are sung. The evening usually concludes with special foods, refreshments, and perhaps a piñata for children.

The *posadas* are special plays which incarnate a Gospel story. They are lived prayer which young and old share together. In some places, because of the cold climate which prohibits an outdoor celebration, the church becomes the home for the community. In this adaptation the different vestibule doors become the inns, and the various roles are taken by different members of the parish family. The prayers on this night are led by the *rezadores* or those members of the community who know the hymns and special prayers by heart. It is possible to augment the ritual with short passages from the Gospel and perhaps a brief reflection by a catechist, deacon or priest. Doing so helps transform this traditional retelling of a quaint religious story into a revelation of the Spirit's presence among us. In some places small ecclesial communities which have formed in various neighborhoods make the *posadas* their own. Gathering inside the homes of the local faithful, children hold painted poles which now represent the doors of the inn. More emphasis is placed on proclaiming the word, as is characteristic of such neighborhood based communities, which helps underline the true significance of the coming feasts for the participating families.

On Christmas Eve the entrance rites of the Eucharistic liturgy can become the last stage of the *posada*. The people gathered in the church sing the traditional hymns which again celebrate the journey of the pilgrims and joyfully open the doors of the hearts to welcome them once more. The Gospel is an invitation to be pilgrims as well, journeying to hear and see the living word. And in the end, all are led to another prepared fiesta: food and drink which manifest the incarnate gift of God, shared with all this Christmas Eve.

Related to the *posadas* is a special Puerto Rican custom called the *parrandas*. This ritual tradition begins just prior to Christmas and concludes on the feast of the Three Kings. Its own contribution of hymns, home visitations, and special foods also allows various familial traditions to be integrated with the ongoing celebration of the Christmas season, especially highlighting the feast of the Epiphany.

## *QUINCE AÑOS*

The celebration of the fifteenth birthday in a young woman's life is a potentially important catechetical moment for her family as well as for the other young people who celebrate with her. Conversely, however, perhaps no other Hispanic celebration has the same potential for eliciting such sharp criticism from priest and people alike as the *quince años*. The focus of such criticism is often the financial excess of these events in families of limited means, who nonetheless desire to provide a memorable celebration for the young woman. Despite the potential difficulties of this celebration, however, it is true that this family custom provides a rich opportunity for engaging the faithful and proclaiming the good news. Few works recognize this potential as well as Angela Everia's classic *La Quinceañera*, which discusses both the necessary catechesis prior to the celebration as well as the ritual of the day itself.

A proper celebration of *quince años* presumes a gathering of the participating young people beforehand. This gathering, which can take the form of a mini-retreat, is not primarily for the sake of input, but is a time of sharing. This is an ideal opportunity to encourage the young people to speak about their lives, their faith, and their doubts. It is also an opportunity to tell again the stories of how this custom originated, and what it can mean for us today. Such a gathering can allow the young to express their opinions about the Church, and at the same time can challenge them to live their faith according to their customs and the call of the Church. This vocational responsibility can be symbolized in the preparation of these youthful participants to be readers and singers, ministers of communion and welcomers at the approaching celebration. In another session the parents and perhaps the compadres of the *quinceañera* can be encouraged and guided to compose their own prayer of gratitude for the daughter and family. Such preparation can, in the short run, enable them to witness their faith at this celebration, and in the long run deepen their commitment to celebrate the ongoing proclamation of the Gospel in the midst of their family. Throughout this preparation of friends and family the young woman herself needs to reflect upon her developing Christian commitment to family and community as she takes this important step toward adulthood. She should be prepared, through personal reflection and dialogue with her family and pastoral team, to make an offering or contribution to the community. This is not meant to be a financial donation, but some gift of herself for the betterment of her family, her community, and herself, such as a commitment to finish her high school education or to become involved in teaching catechism to the children of the parish.

Like other sacramental moments, the ritual itself can be celebrated as a rite of passage: passage from childhood to adulthood, from passivity to participation, from recipient to giver. With parents and godparents at her side, surrounded by her friends, she is handed the candle lit from the Easter candle, renews her baptismal vows, clearly proclaims her offering, and signs herself with baptismal water. The *quinceañera* also receives Hispanic symbols of faith from the community—a medal of the Virgin, a prayer book, rosary, and a ring of promise—and she is affirmed as an example of the young in this parish who are willing to give more of themselves for the good of family and church.

## NOVENARIO

It is with an embrace and the words "Te acompano en tus sentimientos" (I am with you in your grief) that the consolation of grieving is begun. Death is an experience which we all share, and for the Hispanic community it is a special time where tears, *abrazos*, and prayer all come together. It is a moment which everyone in the family and in the extended family share—a time for food and drink provided in abundance by neighbors and friends. Everyone takes a turn. Everyone has a turn.

The rites provided by the Church for the grieving process are a special opportunity for incorporating our heritage. The official ministers of the Church along with the *rezador(a)* guide this process. The wake service, for example, could be structured around the recitation of the Rosary which the *rezador(a)* leads. There are particular prayers at the end of each decade, and after the Rosary a specific response to the Marian litany needs to be offered for the deceased. Integrating appropriate hymns and brief, litany length scriptural passages into this Rosary service further enriches such traditional prayer with key elements of the Church's official liturgy.

Closing intercessions and blessing of the body with holy water effectively bring the wake to a close while offering a ritual link to the funeral Mass itself.

Throughout the ritual process it is important to continue speaking the various names of the living and the dead who hold a special place in the heart of the grieving community. This includes naming the deceased, the dead relatives of the deceased, living family members, and all the patron saints, from that of the town where this life began to that of the church and cemetery where the earthly journey comes to an end. These are the names which will be remembered by the family, who will continue this prayer in the days and months ahead. An important focus during this prayer is the *altarcito*, a small altar which Hispanic families traditionally set aside as a special place of blessing and prayer. The picture of the deceased is enshrined here and a candle, entrusted to the family by a representative of the parish, can be lit during each prayer gathering.

For nine nights following the burial relatives and friends will gather in the family home for the *novenario*. The traditional content of this family novena is, again, the Rosary and Marian litany, which are led by the *rezador(a)*. This custom of Rosary and litany, however, can simply and effectively be combined with another traditional prayer, namely, vespers, which is the Church's evening prayer of praise and intercession. Beginning at the *altarcito* with the lighting of the candle which was originally lit from the Easter candle and presented to the family at the funeral Mass, the *novenario* could then continue with a traditional Hispanic hymn like "Resucito." The recitation of the Rosary could provide the basic framework for the rest of vespers, employing the five decades of the Rosary like the traditional five psalms of evening prayer. Each set of ten "Aves" could be concluded by selected verses from the psalms. The Marian canticle normally sung at vespers, that is, the Magnificat or "O María, Madre Mía," could easily follow. An abbreviated litany of intercession, concluding prayer and sign of peace would bring the service to a close. Such a novena of vespers could effectively combine the official prayer of the Church with traditional Hispanic prayer and put both at the service of those who grieve.

Each of these Hispanic traditions, the *posadas*, *quince años* and *novenario* are seasonal or occasional examples of the kind of cultural and liturgical integration which needs to occur not only at such special times but on the ordinary Sunday gatherings of the community. In some ways Sunday worship —like these specific examples—exists in a world of its own. With its own rules and rhythms, it is a somewhat spontaneous and constantly changing experience. Hispanic worship runs on its own time, namely, when the people have gathered rather than when the clock has struck the appropriate hour. It moves with the freedom of the dance and not always according to the prescribed plan and predetermined order. It has its own spirit which, when respected, bursts forth with an enviable vitality, but can be stifled or quenched by inflexible attitudes. Hispanic worship is not random or chaotic, but it is alive and responsive to the moment. Our adaptations should be similarly responsive.

# 5

# GUIDELINES FOR CULTURAL SENSITIVITY: HISPANICS IN THE UNITED STATES

*ELISA RODRIGUEZ, SC AND GELASIA MARQUEZ*

1.  Family ministers ought to apply themselves to understand the situations within which marriage and family are living today, in order to fulfill their task of serving.

     a. Pope John Paul II and the National Conference of Bishops of the U.S. have recognized:

        1.  The multicultural composition of the Church;
        2.  The inalienable dignity of every human person, irrespective of racial, ethnic, cultural, or national origin or religious beliefs as well as the unity of the human family; and
        3.  How the differences between the members of the Church should be used to strengthen unity, rather than serve as a cause of division. (*Origins* 18.29)

     b. In our ethnically diverse U.S. Catholic Church, where there is no primary ethnic group numerically, the consideration of ethnicity and culture as essential components of family life structure and interactions is determinant in developing programs, policies, and services.

     c. These principles are important when ministering culturally different families:

        1.  Family differences must be understood rather than interpreted and evaluated—what is considered "peculiar" behavior in one cultural setting may be viewed as proper and necessary in another culture.

2. Common experiences/variables that apply to all families must be identified and studied under the umbrella of general characteristics, thus, main areas of differences can be categorized and the varying values and customs of each ethnic group can be highlighted;

3. Family ministers must have sensitivity and flexibility to discover and to understand the "uniqueness" of each family situation as a result of its own history, structural characteristics, ethnic and racial heritage, socioeconomic status, level of acculturation to the mainstream culture of each one of its members, etc.; and finally

4. We can not equate "optimal family functioning" and levels of family life satisfaction with the presence of so-called "strengths"—or positive characteristics, nor with absence of "negative" features but with the ability of individual family members to fulfill their own psycho-social developmental tasks and with the ability of the family itself to re-arrange its own structure, to work-out its transactional patterns and to re-negotiate its dynamics so family continues performing its tasks as well as insures some sense of historical continuity and its own culture and ethnic traditions.

2.    The number of Hispanic families increased by 59% from 1980 to 1989. By the year 2080, Hispanics are expected to number 59.6 million. Therefore, Hispanics (Latinos) in the United States make up a significant part of American society and the Church. Hispanics (Latinos) are from many nations and from a variety of cultures.

a. Hispanics (Latinos) with a long history in the United States.

1. Spanish Americans, descendants of Spanish settlers during the colonization of the Southwest by Spain.

2. Mexican Americans, descendants of Mexican citizens residing in the Southwestern and Western states at the time of the Texas Revolution and the Mexican American War.

These immigrant descent families have retained not only their identification for many generations after immigration but also their ethnic values (Greeley).

b. Hispanic (Latino) immigrants to the United States.

1. Mexican Americans, descendants of Mexican immigrants, residents and/or naturalized citizens.
2. Puerto Ricans
3. Cuban Americans, residents and/or naturalized citizens.
4. Dominican Americans, residents and/or naturalized citizens from the Dominican Republic.
5. Central American immigrants and descendants from the following countries:
   a) Costa Rica
   b) El Salvador
   c) Guatemala
   d) Honduras
   e) Nicaragua
   f) Panama
6. South American immigrants and descendants from the following countries:
   a) Argentina
   b) Bolivia
   c) Chile
   d) Colombia
   e) Ecuador
   f) Paraguay
   g) Uruguay
   h) Venezuela

These immigrant families may belong to one of these two major groups:

1. The recently arrived families—family energy is spent largely on the development of basic survival skills for work, housing, and relating in the new land; and
2. Families with immigrant parents and American born children or immigrant children who are being raised and/or educated in America.

This second group of families experience a great degree of cultural conflict between parents and children. The perception of these conflicts and its internal factors is also affected by where in the acculturative continuum the family members are located.

c. There has been a steady immigration of Hispanics to this country due to economic, religious, and political reasons. Regretfully we cannot assume that all Hispanic families migrated to the U.S. in a planned fashion, or in optimal conditions. Therefore:

1. Members who migrated at different points in their life may have different definitions of who and what they are due to the fact that a person who migrates during adolescence or later, came with a particular value system and psychological frame of mind imposed by the language, educational system, and the historical, cultural, and political trends of their native country (Rodriguez & Villa);
2. Previous life cycle issues may not get adequately resolved or are still pending; and
3. The family life growth cycle may be stopped or interrupted to deal with specific, urgent issues, such as procuring housing, work, learning a language, etc.

d. Hispanics are not only diverse in places of origin but also very diverse culturally, racially, socially, and politically, even from within the same national group, so it is impossible to categorize them in general.

3. Hispanics have come to this country at various times in history and for varied reasons.

 a. Given the diversity of geographical origins, languages, backgrounds, norms, socioeconomic status, and immigration status in developing programs, policies, and services, special attention must be given to assess:

 1. Migration patterns: migration occurs for diverse reasons, and the adjustment of the family depends on the extent to which its original expectations compare with present reality and whether it has a positive connotation or not.

 2. Country of origin: its political, economic, and educational situation. The Mexican migration may be seen as a natural outgrowth of moving to areas that Mexicans perceive to be culturally theirs; Central American immigrants usually migrate as a means of running away from their countries in civil war or in poverty struggles but they are unable to benefit from main institutions due to their undocumented status; Puerto Ricans do not need any documentation to enter or exit from this country, therefore, their pattern of migration reflects repeated ruptures, reinstatement, and a dismantling of familial and communal networks (Garcia-Preto); finally Cubans' sense of temporary uprootedness helped them to develop a "frozen" culture in which energies were spent not in acculturation but in maintaining the values/morals of the homeland.

 3. Age and developmental stage of family members at the time of migration in order to understand what experiences are stored in which language (Inclan);

 4. Socioeconomic status and educational background of family members prior to migration—although a poor person may have a sense of pride about previous achievements and life styles that may be more influential than their current status; and

 5. Availability of support systems—especially friends, church, and ethnic group.

4. Hispanics have very deep cultural roots in the United States.

    a. Hispanics were preceded in occupying this country only by Native Americans.

    b. In one way or another Hispanics are within two different cultural environments and are dealing in one way or another with a process of acculturation.

    c. The process of acculturation involves the whole life of the child/adolescent/young adult/adult, therefore, Hispanic families are in continuous need of doing a selective adaptation and undergoing a process of differentiation in order:

        1. To make decisions and choices for a healthy accommodation to two different socio-economic-cultural contexts and

        2. For their internal identity adjustment in ways of thinking, feeling, and acting.

    d. Different modes of adaptation of migrant ethnic families have been described. Common patterns observed are the following:

        1. Denigrating the old culture—some families sever the old ties and deny their cultural origin by adopting the external features of a stereotyped American family. Habits and perceived values—often materialistic—are copied;

        2. Denying the new culture—families turn inward, associating only with members of their own background and attempting to reproduce a micro-culture similar to the one in the home country. However, the children in these families, due to contact with the outside world through schools and friends, become acculturated and conflicts frequently develop in the next generation; and

        3. Becoming able to bring the two cultures together and tolerate the conflict and anxiety of crossing

cultural boundaries. Important attachments to ethnic culture maintained along with a productive adjustment to the host culture.

e. For many Hispanic families the immigration and adaptation process is a painful one:

1. Many of them must go "from extended to nuclear families, from group existence to individual existence, as they lose their roots through migration; as church, religion and community become unfamiliar and unresponsive" (Paredes).

2. Families are often caught in a state of helplessness without appropriate support systems. Resources that they would have relied on in home countries are often not found in the United States, while the existing resources may appear alien to them. In addition to various adaptational problems faced by legal immigrants, illegal aliens encounter a number of obvious social, psychological, and legal problems.

f. Family coping mechanisms are particularly threatened by poverty and discrimination (Minuchin). A great number of Hispanic families live on poverty levels, they are more vulnerable to disease, lower self esteem, have daily stresses that are quite pervasive and negatively influence their children.

g. The loss of ability to use native language and a corresponding greater fluency in English on the part of the children generates poor communication between generations. Also children become the main source of guidance, control, and decision making when they have to translate for their parents when developmentally they are unprepared to handle those duties.

5. As members of a minority group, Hispanics have experienced:

a. Being ignored

   b. Being taken advantage of

   c. Being pushed out of school, jobs

   d. Being slighted, ridiculed, harassed

   e. Being overworked, underpaid, underemployed, etc.

   f. Being considered ignorant because of language difficul-
      ties

Hispanics have responded in various ways to this oppression:

   a. By giving in to the societal pressure to assimilate and
      have changed their names, given up all traces of
      cultural differences.

   b. By assuming some of the dominant cultural values, but
      not all. Keeping those values which are important to
      family and community.

   c. By gathering into neighborhoods (barrios) where they
      can be themselves without outside interference, i.e.,
      basically rejecting society's efforts to assimilate them.

   d. By entering a process of re-evaluation which often
      leads them to reclaim their lost cultural values and
      traditions.

   In developing programs, policies, and services for Hispanic families, leaders need to understand the different levels and
processes that families go through in their adjustment to the
host culture and respect the place where people are without
making assumptions or being judgmental while taking positive
steps towards creating an environment of healing and acceptance.

6.   The fundamental institutions for Hispanics are God,
family, and community.

   a. Hispanics have no doubt about "God who cares" and
      around this belief they develop their practices and
      spiritual values.

b. Hispanics tend to personalize their relationship with God and the saints. Mary, the saints, and souls in purgatory are members of their extended family. Hispanics argue with them, ask them favors, tell them jokes, include them in popular songs, keep pictures or images of them alongside of the portraits of the family and best friends.

c. Faith has made Hispanics a joyful and providentialistic people. In their fiestas they celebrate the mystery life that, in its successes and failures, joy and sadness, birth and even death, is a gift from God.

d. Religiosity also gives Hispanics a more spiritual dimension in life. Hispanics emphasize spiritual values and are willing to sacrifice material satisfaction for spiritual goals. For them being is more important than doing or having.

e. The family is the foremost institution in Hispanic culture. For Hispanics, family includes not only relatives by blood and marriages, but also relatives by association such as godparents, relatives by friendship and out of respect such as other hometown or elderly neighbors.

f. The family is the first school of love, tenderness, acceptance, discipline, and respect. In their homes, Hispanics have come to experience the bonds of friendship, mutual support, concern for one another, and the presence of God. In times of stress, Hispanics turn to their families for help; their cultural expectation is that when a family member is experiencing a crisis or has a problem, others in the family are obligated to help, especially those who are in stable positions.

g. Hispanic families enmesh their members in a system of helpgiving exchanges which has the force of a sacred obligatory norm; it is sustained by the double edge of guilt and gratitude. That is, not to help a relative in need evokes feelings of sinful guilt; in turn, to be helped by a relative induces feelings of gratitude. The norm applies through time because the person is bound permanently to his or her family of origin. The norm applies also through space, because relatives who are separated by geographical distance behave in accordance with what they have learned.

h. Celebrations of life stages are cherished by Hispanics and these form significant Church-family events. Some of these are baptisms, first communions, quinceañeras, weddings, and funerals.

i. Mutual help and a sense of hospitality crisscross blood and affinal relationships to include neighbors, friends, and the community at large fostering principles of true solidarity among Hispanics.

7.   The fundamental values of Hispanics differ significantly from the values of the dominant society.

a. Whereas dominant culture values constant activity, control of oneself, of others, of nature, Hispanics practice passive acceptance, seek harmony within oneself, among others, and with nature.

b. Whereas the dominant culture espouses planning and efficiency (business), Hispanics value spontaneity and the personal (friendships).

c. Whereas the dominant culture values "having" (possessions) and promotes materialism, pragmatism and technical progress, Hispanics value "being" (communion) having human relationships, beauty, and tradition.

d. Whereas the dominant culture views success in terms of upward mobility of the individual and admires ambition, motivation, and competition, Hispanics view success as stability of the group, and admires stability in a person, perseverance, and cooperation.

e. Whereas the dominant culture determines that respect is due to those who earn it, Hispanics understand that respect is due because a person exists.

8. In communicating, Hispanics visualize and experience the world as a totality using symbols, gestures, sounds, dance, poetry, music. They communicate in indirect and discrete ways which often include a great deal of diplomacy. Hispanics prefer to communicate person to person.

In conclusion, in developing programs, policies, and services leaders need to be sensitive to the strength and inspiration of Hispanic Christian values.

## WORKS CITED

Garcia-Preto, N. *Puerto-Rican Families. Ethnicity and Family Therapy*. Ed. M. McGoldrick, J. Pearce, and J. Giordano. New York: Guilford Press, 1982.

Inclan, J. "Variations in Value Orientations in Mental Health Work with Puerto Rican Clients." *Psychotherapy*, 22.2: 325–334.

Minuchin, S. *Family and Family Therapy*. Cambridge, MA: Harvard University Press, 1974.

Paredes, Mario. "Ministering to the Migrant and Alien Families," The Bishop and the Family—The Church Addresses Her Future, 1985 Workshop.

# 6

# GUIDELINES FOR CULTURAL SENSITIVITY: PACIFIC ASIAN AMERICANS

## DAVID NG

1.  Contemporary North American church and society are multicultural.

   a. Church and society are no longer a "melting pot" into which all racial, ethnic, and national groups are blended into a single culture.

   b. Church and society are no longer monocultural societies into which minority groups are assimilated into the majority group (minority racial and ethnic groups assimilated into the majority white group).

   c. Church and society today can move toward a "mosaic," or "tapestry," or "tossed salad" form of society in which many diverse groups are included in the whole but continue to maintain their individual group identity and culture.

   d. Pacific Asian Americans (or, Pacific Asian North Americans, if Canadians are included) are a part of the multicultural society which is a "mosaic."

   e. Pacific Asian Americans are numerically a minority group in North America but they have equal status with every racial/ethnic group in the multicultural society.

   Therefore, in developing programs, policies, and services, leaders need to affirm our multicultural society and avoid any implication that one racial, ethnic, or cultural group is superior to the others.

2. Pacific Asian Americans are themselves multicultural and diverse.

   a. Pacific Asian Americans could be described or categorized in various ways, for example, by region and national origin:

      1. Pacific Islands
         a) Filipino Americans
         b) Hawaiian Americans
         c) Samoan Americans
         d) Tongan Americans
         e) Micronesian Americans (such as Marshallese, Palauans, etc.)
         f) Other islands, such as Guam, Midway
      2. East Asian
         a) Indian (East Indian Americans)
         b) Pakistani Americans
      3. Asian
         a) Japanese Americans
         b) Chinese Americans
         c) Korean Americans
         d) Taiwanese Americans
         e) Okinawan Americans
      4. Southeast Asian
         a) Vietnamese Americans
         b) Cambodian Americans
         c) Thai Americans
         d) Burmese (Myamar) Americans
         e) Hmong Americans

   b. Pacific Asian Americans, because of their diversity, cannot be categorized or described easily, using only one frame of reference or one physical, social, psychological, historical, or religious stereotype.

Therefore, in developing programs, policies, and services, leaders need to affirm the variety of nationalities, cultures, and experiences among Pacific Asian Americans, and avoid treating all of them in a monocultural, stereotypical fashion.

3. Pacific Asian Americans have had a variety of experiences of immigration.

   a. Some Pacific Asian Americans are the third, fourth, fifth, or later generation in North America. Some of these Pacific Asian Americans are thoroughly assimilated into American culture.

   b. Some Pacific Asian Americans are first generation, may be recent immigrants, and may have only a small degree of assimilation into the North American culture. Some speak only their native language and not English.

   c. There are a variety of reasons for Pacific Asian American immigration into North America, including poverty, education, economic opportunity (wealth), politics, and family. Not all Pacific Asian Americans are wealthy or have skills in business.

   Therefore, in developing programs, policies, and services, leaders need to be aware of the variety of reasons why Pacific Asian Americans are in North America, and be particularly sensitive to those who are having difficulty adjusting to a culture that is different for them.

4. Pacific Asian Americans have experienced a variety of national approaches to assimilation, such as:

   a. Cultural annihilation (slavery, genocide, etc.)

   b. Cultural alienation (segregation)

   c. Cultural substitution (rejecting one's own culture)

   d. Cultural assimilation (adopting the majority culture)

   e. Cultural accommodation (being tolerated by the majority culture)

   Therefore, in developing programs, policies, and services, leaders need to be aware of the North American society's and the Church's blemished history of race, culture, and ethnic relations. Leaders need to foster creative, positive efforts aimed at developing an accepting and harmonious multicultural society.

5. Pacific Asian Americans continue to experience condescension, racism, and institutional racism.

   a. Some Pacific Asian Americans find it difficult to trust persons and institutions of the majority culture.

   b. Some Pacific Asian Americans prefer to associate primarily or only with their own ethnic or national group.

   c. Some Pacific Asian Americans will participate in activities with other ethnic groups only when someone from their group facilitates the participation.

   Therefore, in developing programs, policies, and services, leaders need to be sensitive to the possibility that some Pacific Asian Americans have endured prejudice against them and may still harbor painful memories or feelings about how they have been treated by other persons and groups in North America. To develop trusting relationships with Pacific Asian Americans who have been hurt by prejudice will require patience, understanding, tact, and a willingness to listen to Pacific Asian American persons.

6. Pacific Asian Americans can be "assimilated" through a process of cultural pluralism that assumes church and society to be multicultural and all racial/ethnic groups to be a part of the general society while maintaining individual cultural identity.

   Therefore, in developing programs, policies, and services, leaders need to develop and exhibit an affirmative attitude about multicultural society, and be creative in incorporating into existing and new programs positive experiences of multicultural activities and learnings.

7. Pacific Asian American families may be quite different than Euro-American families. Pacific Asian Americans may exhibit

male-dominant, patriarchal family and group relational patterns, but for differing reasons.

a. Some Asian groups follow Confucian values and social relationship patterns that emphasize respect for elders, respect for (or reverence of) ancestors, filial responsibility, and hierarchical relationships including the superiority of males over females.

b. Some Pacific Island cultures follow values that reflect small village social patterns such as the authority of the chief, the superiority of males over females, and the village as an "extended family."

c. Most Pacific Asian American cultures emphasize family membership and loyalty. The role of the individual is established in the context of the family, and decisions are made with family expectations in mind.

d. The roles of children and adolescents differ between Pacific Asian American cultures (and differ from the roles in majority American culture).

For example, children and adolescents in some Pacific Asian American cultures have few rights and must accept the authority of elders, particularly the father. Unlike the freedom of expression afforded in majority American culture, many Pacific Asian American young people are not to make independent decisions or commitments. School and career choices are to be made in light of family expectations and needs.

e. Pacific Asian American adolescents often face "double and triple stress" as adolescents, as racial/ethnic minority persons, and as persons caught in cultural clash. They need help in being "bi-cultural" or "amphibious."

f. Pacific Asian American families often need help or extra understanding regarding family relationships and family life. They may not be able to do the same activities expected of majority American culture families, because of language difficulties, different cultural values, and different ways of expressing roles and authority in families.

Therefore, in developing programs, policies, and services, leaders need to take into account a wide range of attitudes and actions of Pacific Asian American families, such as their original cultures and traditions, experiences of immigration, strategies for assimilation, communities for residence, economic status, religious commitments, relationship between parents and children, etc.

Leaders often need to be understanding of the cultural conflicts often experienced by Pacific Asian American families. Particularly those with young persons.

8.   Pacific Asian Americans tend to be communal rather than individualistic.

    a. They tend to establish their identities in relation to the family or group.

    b. The peace and harmony of the family or group is viewed as more important than individual happiness.

Therefore, in developing programs, policies, and services, leaders can affirm the sense of corporateness and interrelatedness of Pacific Asian Americans and understand and appreciate the different values that inform and motivate them.

9.   Pacific Asian Americans often practice styles of thinking that are different than "Western styles of thinking."

    a. Pacific Asian Americans do not necessarily prefer rational, logical, scientific styles of thinking; some (perhaps many) have been brought up with preferences for intuitive thinking, acceptance of mystery and non-rationality, and a mixture of subjective and objective thinking.

    b. Affective and global thinking is practiced, in contrast to cognitive and detailed or analytical thinking favored in Western cultures.

c. Objective, factual information is not necessarily separated from personal, subjective feelings. Thinking and learning may be impressionistic or aesthetic, or holistic.

Therefore, in developing programs, policies, and services, leaders need to be sensitive to the different forms of expression and different styles of thinking that are a part of the rich, varied ways of thinking and acting among Pacific Asian Americans.

10. Pacific Asian Americans often practice styles of communication that are different than "Western styles of communication."

a. Communication often is formal or formalized, and mindful of protocol.

b. Some communication is indirect and contextual, and seems ambiguous to those who are accustomed to precision and directness.

c. Personal feelings may be suppressed.

d. Especially among Asian Americans, body contact is avoided as well as eye contact.

e. Especially among first generation Asian Americans, a show of affection may be avoided.

f. Deference is seen as a virtue rather than a weakness.

g. Oral tradition and story forms are preferred over written forms and fact-based forms, by some Pacific Asian Americans, especially Pacific Islanders.

Therefore, in developing programs, policies, and services, leaders can be appreciative to the variety of styles of life and ways of thinking exhibited by Pacific Asian Americans, and can encourage them to share their differences as gifts to the entire group.

11. Pacific Asian American religious tradition does not necessarily reflect Judeo-Christian tradition.

   a. Pacific Asian American religious tradition will reflect historical, regional, and cultural tradition, and is as diverse as are Pacific Asian American cultures.

   b. For example, Pacific Asian American cultures have observed and practiced Islamic, Christian, Buddhist, Shinto, shamanist, Hindu, animalistic, and other religious traditions, and Taoist or Confucian philosophies.

   c. Within families there may be conflicts over the practice of religious rituals and celebrations.

   d. Pacific Asian American parents may expect their children to observe certain religious rituals and celebrations, in order to preserve cultural values and traditions.

   e. Some Pacific Asian Americans will view Christianity as a "Western religion."

   f. Not all Pacific Asian Americans are committed to a religion or particularly to Christianity.

   g. Some Pacific Asian Americans, including many Chinese, Koreans, and Japanese, maintain Confucian social values and ethics. For them religion and social ethics are parallel areas of life and religion does not necessarily require commitment and corporate membership in the same ways they are required in Christianity.

   h. Many Pacific Asian American families include members who practice different faiths or belong to different denominations.

   For example, a family may include parents who are Buddhists, children who are Baptists, Roman Catholics, and non-religious. Such families may not be able to do any religious activities together or discuss Christian concepts together.

Therefore, in developing programs, policies, and services, leaders need to be sensitive to the variety of religious expression that may be present in a Pacific Asian American family and to feelings of conflict or confusion that are sometimes experienced. In presenting the Christian faith leaders need to be clear, loving, and humble; they need to be open-minded about religious truth and to non-western forms of Christianity.

# 7

# GUIDELINES FOR CULTURAL SENSITIVITY: NATIVE AMERICANS

## *MICHAEL GALVAN*

1.   North American society provides a multicultural context for the experience of the Roman Catholic Church.

   a. Assimilation is no longer the guiding principle among the various racial, ethnic, and national groups in our society.

   b. The preservation and practice of one's own culture, traditions, and languages are a primary value.

   c. North American society is a blend of various groups: each maintaining their own identity while producing a North American tapestry.

   d. Native Americans hold a unique place in this tapestry as the original inhabitants of this land.

   e. While Native Americans are a minority, their cultures, languages, and traditions have equal value with other racial/ethnic groups in a multicultural society.

   f. The Roman Catholic Church exists in this multicultural society.

The value and integrity of all racial, ethnic, and cultural groups must be respected. North American society is not the assimilation of all groups into one but the experience of a community of communities.

2.   Native Americans are diverse in their own cultures and traditions.

    a. The primary identification of Native Americans is with their village, tribe, or nation.

    b. North of the Rio Grande, there are over 300 extant Native languages and cultures.

    c. The cultural differences among Native Peoples are as diverse as other cultural groups, such as Europeans and Asians.

Native Peoples must be viewed through their own cultural tapestry. Programs must avoid an attempt to present a monocultural understanding of Native Americans.

3.    Native Americans have had a variety of experiences of European contact.

    a. Some Native Americans had their initial European contact almost 500 years ago. Others have had substantial contact only in the last 150 years.

    b. The experience of European contact varied partially because of the different European groups (English, French, Spanish, Russian) and their different approaches to colonization.

    c. A number of Native American Peoples had their primary European contacts with Americans of European descent who no longer considered themselves to be immigrants.

    d. The experience of initial conversion to Catholic Christianity also differs from over 400 years to less than 100 years.

The variety of Native American histories with Europeans needs to be taken into account in programs and policies.

4.    Native Americans have a diversity of experiences of living in a multicultural society.

a. Some Native Americans live among their own people on their own land (reservations).

b. Some Native Americans have grown up on their reservations and have migrated to an urban setting. For most, this is a real and dramatic experience of immigration.

c. Many urban Native Americans (who constitute at least half of the Native population) maintain some contact with their cultures through urban Native Centers and/or visits to their reservations.

d. In urban areas, there will be Native Americans who are native to the area and others who have migrated there from other parts of North America.

e. Not all Native Americans have reservations. Some urban Natives belong to landless tribes. Their primary community is the multicultural urban experience of North American society.

The variety of reasons why Native Americans live where they do in our society needs to be understood and appreciated. Programs need to reflect their pluralistic experience.

5.   Native Americans have a variety of experiences in regard to their own culture and the dominant North American culture.

a. After European contact, a number of Native American tribes lost their cultures and language through the destruction of their villages. Some tribes disappeared while others continued with a few survivors.

b. Through the experience of Christian missionization, some Native Americans lost their own culture and language and adopted European ones.

c. Some Native Americans maintained a strictly divided two cultural life: one for the village or reservation and the other for the larger society and often for the Church.

d. Some Native Americans have lost their culture and language because of the governmental assimilation efforts of previous years.

e. There is presently a revival of Native cultures, traditions, and languages occurring. Many are regaining their culture.

The many diverse ways in which Native Americans relate to their own societies and to North American society must be appreciated in any program.

6.   Native Americans continue to experience racial stereotyping and racism.

a. Through centuries of contact, certain stereotypes have developed around Native Americans. The media has played a significant role in dispersing and supporting these stereotypes.

b. Native Americans experience among themselves various forms of racism through tribal prejudices.

c. Due to the experience of reservations, Native Peoples have known the experience of forced segregation. The reservation system developed as a consequence of the Native Peoples being a conquered people.

d. Some Native Americans have a mistrust of the institutions of the dominant culture, e.g., governmental agencies, church.

The reality of centuries of prejudice, racial stereotypes, and racism needs to be acknowledged. Programs need to develop and support trusting relationships between Native Americans and the larger North American society.

7.   Among Native Americans, the understanding of relationships provides some shared elements and a means to embrace them in a pluralistic society.

a. Native Americans arrive at their self-identity through the various relationships in which they share.

b. How Native Americans experience these primary relationships will help an understanding of a particular cultural group. These relationships are with word, time, land, and all creatures.

c. Native Americans view themselves as living through these relationships in a sacred and spiritual world.

Programs need to appreciate the deeply spiritual world of Native Americans. An understanding of Native Peoples' primary relationships will be of help in this area.

8. Native relationship with word.

a. The spoken word has a higher value than the written word. The use of story has primary importance since through the telling of one's tribe's stories, the people are given and sustained in life.

b. The speaker's personal integrity gives credence and value to the words he or she speaks.

c. The value of words lessens with their quantity. Some Native Americans may appear reticent when in fact they are respecting the value of the conversation.

d. Silence has an intrinsic value. It is important to spend time in silence with people.

Any program must appreciate the Native relationship with word and must rely more on the spoken word than on the written word.

9. Native relationship with time.

a. The primary understanding of time is how it relates to the days, months, seasons of the world. Time is the expression of one's unity and harmony with the world.

b. While the understanding of time used in the dominant society by hours and minutes has importance, it is secondary to the Native understanding of time.

   c. Through the use of ritual, one can place oneself more in harmony with the rhythm of the world. History is not seen as linear but rather as how it reflects the movement of the world, of the seasons.

   d. Through the respect for one's elders, this appreciation of one's history is reflected. For the elders carry in their bodies the traditions and values of the people.

The Native understanding of time needs to be appreciated to avoid confusion. History is not viewed as a chronicle of past events but rather a reflection of living with the universe.

10. Native relationship with land.

   a. Native Americans view the world on which we live as Mother Earth: the giver and sustainer of our life.

   b. In the faith expression of Native Americans, Catholic Christianity needs to be inculturated in the Native traditions and cultures. Otherwise, the adoption of Catholic Christianity would mean the loss of one's culture.

   c. Native spirituality and Catholic Christianity are compatible with one another.

Catholic Christianity needs to be inculturated in the various Native traditions and cultures which are deeply spiritual. Such an approach reflects the acceptance of the pluralistic world in which we live.

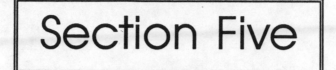

# Section Five

# FAMILY AND PARISH RITUALS: MAKING THE CONNECTIONS

# ESSAY:
# PARISH CELEBRATIONS
# WITH A FAMILY PERSPECTIVE

## *THOMAS BRIGHT*

The lives of families and parishes are tightly intertwined. Neither can fulfill its task of proclaiming and promoting God's kingdom in the contemporary world without the other. Mutual support and encouragement are essential. Parishes simply would not exist without the families that people them and provide them with their unique personalities. Families, on the other hand, need the parish community to help them connect with a story of faith and commitment that is broader than their own experience.

Parish prayer and ritual celebrations are a key arena in which the lives of the faith community and the family connect. If parish celebrations are planned and carried out with a sensitivity to family concerns, commitments, and capabilities they will be growthful for all involved. There are many ways of connecting parish and family around ritual and prayer. Consider the following:

1. Encourage reflection on what it means to be the "domestic church" or "church of the home." How are families called to live out the Gospel mandate today? What do prayer and ritual have to do with proclaiming the Gospel message?

2. Raise the awareness of the parish community to the need for family prayer and ritual. How is family prayer different from the prayer of the wider church community? Where do family and parish prayer and ritual connect?

3. Connect families with an interest in family prayer and ritual. Encourage families to share what they pray about as a family, and how. What opportunities does the parish

provide for families to come together for sharing and support? How central a concern is family prayer and ritual in these gatherings?

4. Provide prayer resources for families. Expand the ways families pray by providing them with resources that feature a variety of content and formats for prayer. Are resource articles or books made available to parish families? Are family prayer suggestions offered on a seasonal or event basis?

5. Critique parish rituals from the perspective of family involvement. How are families involved in the planning or carrying out of parish celebrations? Are family members involved in parish liturgical ministry scheduled as members of a family team or spread across a week's or month's celebrations? What age groups or family structures are targeted in parish celebrations?

6. Critique parish rituals from the perspective of family issues. How central are the life issues of families to parish celebrations? How conscious is the blend between rituals that celebrate the Church's liturgical year and those that celebrate everyday or milestone events in the life of the families in your community?

7. Reflect on the racial, national, and ethnic mix of the families in your faith community. What role do the culture and ethnic traditions of the families in your community play in decisions about what and how you celebrate as a parish community?

The *Catholic Families Series* guidebook, *Family Rituals and Celebrations*, suggests four categories of rituals that provide parishes with an opportunity to work in partnership with families: rituals through the year, family milestone rituals, ethnic rituals and traditions, and family rituals through the day. Each of these approaches will be briefly explored in the pages that follow, and suggestions offered on how these different categories of rites can be celebrated with a family perspective.

# RITUALS THROUGH THE YEAR

The rituals of the Catholic Church provide one of the primary ways in which faith is shared from one generation to the next. The ritual celebrations of the liturgical year offer both a sense of permanence and a sense of possibility—a long-standing tradition of celebrating faith that remains open to meeting new needs and being expressed in new ways. Coupled with civic celebrations like Thanksgiving, Martin Luther King Jr. Day, and Earth Day, Church rituals provide a basis for celebrating faith as parish and family throughout the year. How can parish celebrations of Church and civic events consciously incorporate a family perspective? Several approaches are possible.

Parishes and families can celebrate the same event in the same way. Some rituals can be carried over directly from a parish to a family celebration. The prayers used, for example, in the parish rite of lighting the candles in the Advent wreath can be included verbatim in the parish bulletin and families encouraged to repeat the rite throughout the week. Repetition of the parish rite helps families see that their prayers are shared by others, and recognize their membership in the larger church community.

Parishes and families can celebrate the same event, but in a shortened or adapted form. Some rituals do not lend themselves to a straight transfer from parish to home celebration. Repeating a parish Thanksgiving Day service at home, for example, could prove redundant and leave the table full of cold food. A Thanksgiving Day blessing, incorporated into the parish service, could, however, be repeated to advantage and allow people to "dig in" while the food is still hot.

Parishes can provide families with general prayer resources, or specific worship suggestions, for the different seasons of the Church year and civic holidays.

Parishes can highlight the varied needs and concerns of families through the year, relating them to the appropriate Church or civic holiday. Two examples follow. The first uses the Church feast of Pentecost as a context for recalling and rejoicing in what it means to be Church as parish and as family. The second offers an approach for incorporating a special blessing for fathers into parish Eucharistic celebration on Father's Day.

## PENTECOST SUNDAY CELEBRATION [1]

The following process can be used as part of the homily sharing at a Pentecost Eucharist or at a separate service later in the day.

*Leader*: Please take a few moments to reflect and celebrate the birthday of the Church. Remember how we, as members of both the "church of the home" and the parish community, share in the mission of Jesus. This mission is revealed in our lives through our commitment to others, at home, in our parish, and in the wider community. As members of God's family, we share in the task of making God's love known to those near at hand and far away.

We, the parish faith community of (name of parish), belong to the local Church of the Roman Catholic Diocese of (name of diocese). Like parish members of previous generations, we have entered into a baptismal covenant with our God, and with each other. As members of the church of our home, we have also entered into a similar baptismal covenant. This covenant has bonded us together so intimately that our salvation is dependent upon it. Through this holy covenant we, as a people, have been chosen by God and sent by the Spirit to our generation to love others as our God has loved us in Jesus Christ. We are called to gather, in God's name, both with the parish community and with our families so that we may experience God's presence and love. This intimate relationship with God will sustain us in our mission to love each other faithfully, and unconditionally.

We are therefore committed to:

- open our hearts to God's love for us;

---

[1] The Pentecost Sunday Celebration was contributed by the Rev. Thomas F. Lynch.

- celebrate together our experience of the Risen Lord;
- celebrate the sacredness of our family experiences.

We believe that we have been sent by Jesus and led by the Holy Spirit to:

- love and forgive others as the Lord has loved and forgiven us;
- be just and generous to others as the Lord has gifted us;
- share with others how the Lord has healed us;
- and to lead others to the Lord's love, forgiveness, and healing.

Therefore, we are called to challenge one another to be more loving, forgiving, generous, and just. We are challenged to share all we have (time, talent, and treasure) with one another, especially the poor, so that we may fulfill the mission of Jesus Christ—the one sent to free all people to love and live life fully.

Birthdays are a time to recall, affirm, and dream. I invite you now to recall and share with others:

- your fond memories of the parish community and of your family;
- the ways you are presently involved in building up your parish and family;
- how your parish and family have helped you understand the mission of Jesus and what you are doing to live it out in your life;
- your hopes and dreams for the parish community, and for your family, the "church of the home."

## PARISH AND HOME BLESSING FOR MOTHERS [2]

Celebrated after Communion at the Eucharist on Mother's Day, this blessing will provide an opportunity to offer thanks,

---

[2] The Parish Blessing for Mothers was contributed by the Rev. Thomas F. Lynch.

affirmation, and a special blessing to mothers in the parish. Families have been encouraged to attend Eucharist together.

## THANKSGIVING

*Leader*: Dearest mothers, for saying yes to our lives and for offering us the chance to live and grow.
*Children*: We say, thank you.

*Leader*: For the times we just needed someone to talk to, and you were there.
*Children*: We say, thank you.

*Leader*: For the times no one believed in us, and you stood firmly by us.
*Children*: We say, thank you.

*Leader*: For the times you did so much for us, and expected so little or nothing in return.
*Children*: We say, thank you.

*Leader*: For the times we messed up, and you graciously embraced and forgave us.
*Children*: We say, thank you.

*Leader*: For the times when we were sick, and you gave us your special, loving, and motherly care.
*Children*: We say, thank you.

## AFFIRMATIONS

*Leader*: I invite you now to take a moment to tell your mother about one of her qualities which you admire; if your mother is not here with you, please share your reflections with family or friends seated near you.

When the sharing is completed, a son or daughter now says, on behalf of all the children, the following:

I believe in you Mom. You are someone who is very important to me, not because of the things you do, but rather for the person you are. I respect you and love you. I know in my heart that you are God's gift to me. May

God strengthen the affection we share for each other, and keep us close forever.

**BLESSING**

*Leader*: Lord God, bless our mother this day with all good things: health, joy, love, and laughter. Keep her in your care and protect her from all which is harmful. And grant her peace and justice all her days. Amen.

NOTE: Children can be invited to extend a blessing to their mothers by signing her with the sign of the cross on her forehead. Mothers, likewise, can be invited to extend a similar blessing to their children.

For those mothers who will not be blessed by their children this Mother's Day, the parish community prays a blessing for them.

## *PARISH AND HOME BLESSING FOR FATHERS* [3]

Celebrated after Communion at the Eucharist on Father's Day, this blessing will provide an opportunity to offer thanks, affirmation, and a special blessing to fathers in the parish. Families have been encouraged to attend Eucharist together.

*Leader*: Lord, we have relied on our fathers for so many things throughout the years, and we often forget that he is not invincible, but rather a person who has strengths and weaknesses just like us. Help us Lord, to always give our fathers the chance to be simply who they are, special blessings to us. Lord, this Father's Day may we learn to love and appreciate our fathers, and to bless them with the innocence we once shared with them as children.

---

[3] The Parish Blessing for Fathers was contributed by the Rev. Thomas F. Lynch.

## INTERCESSIONS

*Leader*: Lord, may the fathers among us experience your love for them in new and deeper ways this Father's Day. May they always be aware of how deeply their children love them.
*Children*: Hear us God, our Father.

*Leader*: May we always have fond memories of the time and affection shared with our father.
*Children*: Hear us God, our Father.

*Leader*: May we always have the courage to tell our father how much we love him.
*Children*: Hear us God, our Father.

*Leader*: Free our families from the pain of hurtful words and actions that push people apart, so that we may be united in love.
*Children*: Hear us God, our Father.

*Leader*: May we always walk proudly with our father in times of prosperity and in times of need, and humbly support him as he has supported us.
*Children*: Hear us God, our Father.

## AFFIRMATIONS

*Leader*: I invite you now to take a moment to tell your father about one of his qualities which you admire; if your father is not here with you, please share your reflections with family or friends seated near you.

When the sharing is completed, a son or daughter now says, on behalf of all the children, the following:

I believe in you Dad. You are someone who is very important to me, not because of the things you do, but rather for the person you are. I respect you and love you. I know in my heart that you are God's gift to me. May God strengthen the affection we share for each other, and keep us close forever.

## BLESSING

*Leader*: Lord God, bless our fathers on this special day with all good things: health and love, friends and laughter. Keep them in your care. Give them the strength to continue to share your love and concern with all they meet. Amen.

NOTE: Children can be invited to extend a blessing to their fathers by signing him with the sign of the cross on his forehead. Fathers, likewise, can be invited to extend a similar blessing to their children.

For those fathers who will not be blessed by their children this Father's Day, the parish community prays a blessing for them.

# FAMILY MILESTONE RITUALS

Special moments in the life of the family provide an opportunity to share God's loving presence to families. Milestone events in the life of a family can be exciting (engagement of a son or daughter) or sorrowful (unexpected death of a relative), joyful (burning the mortgage on the family home) or filled with terror (first ride with a newly-licensed driver). In some milestone events, the parish is an almost-automatic partner with families. In others, the parish connection is, at best, faint. All offer an opportunity for parishes to stand with families in moments of celebration, challenge and crisis, offering a word of support and encouragement. A few simple suggestions for parish involvement follow.

Invite families to identify and celebrate the milestone events in their lives as opportunities to understand who God is for them in a new way. Encourage them to make God a conscious companion on their journey through the valleys and hills of family life. Ask families to keep the parish staff and leadership aware of the milestones in their lives so that they can join with them in prayer at these moments.

Be present to families in their milestone moments. The presence of members of the parish leadership team at events

significant in the life of a family (special birthdays or anniversaries, graduations or moments of community recognition)
bears strong witness to their commitment to families and
family ministry. If presence is not possible, consider a quick
note or prayer card sent in the parish's name.

Publicly recognize, and invite the parish community to
join in prayer with, parish members who are celebrating milestone events. While this is a common practice in events of
significance like birth and death, other milestone events are
often forgotten. When, for example, was the last time parish
members were recognized upon retirement from the business
community or on the celebration of an eighteenth birthday and
subsequent registration for the draft? Milestone events can be
included in the general intercessions at liturgy, mentioned in
the parish bulletin or newsletter, etc.

Develop special, periodic parish rituals to celebrate family
milestone events, for example a June Prayer Service and
Reception for all graduates (kindergarten through graduate
school), a parish welcome to new parishioners or farewell to
those moving beyond the parish, recognition of retirees and
first-timers to the job market, etc. Some milestones fall
naturally into the calendar or liturgical year while others will
need more conscious thought if they are to be included.

The following service is an example of parish recognition
of an ordinary, but no-less-miraculous milestone event in
family life—pregnancy. The service, as described, was celebrated during Advent, the season of expectancy, but could
easily be adapted for celebration at other times of the year.

## ADVENT BLESSING FOR EXPECTANT PARENTS [4]

The Advent season provides wonderful opportunities for the
family and parish community to come together for blessings.
On the fourth Sunday of Advent, a blessing for expectant
parents can take place after the homily. The Gospel for the

---

[4] The Advent Blessing for Expectant Parents was contributed by the Rev.
Thomas F. Lynch

fourth Sunday proclaims the pregnancy of Mary. This blessing reminds the communities of the home and parish of the ongoing expectant joy of the coming of the Christ child to humanity. At this blessing, the parents are asked to come forth and stand in front of the community. Community members are asked to extend their right hands as the blessing is prayed by the presider or another community leader.

## CALL TO PRAYER

Dearest God, Father of life, we thank you for inviting these expectant parents to participate in the continuing eternal action of your creation. They realize that nothing can come into existence without the creative touch of your loving hands. They stand before you today in awe and wonder for you have blest their womb with a life that they will love forever.

Dearest God, Mother of creation, hold these parents as tenderly as they will hold their child. Help them to realize that this child has been chosen by you to be the Christ for future generations. Let us welcome this child as a gift from you.

## LITANY OF THANKSGIVING AND PETITION

The community of faith now joins with you, expectant parents, in this litany of thanksgiving and petition. The response will be: Blessed be God, and these parents and children forever.

1. We thank you for the gift of this life (Blessed be God...)
2. We thank you for our gift of love (Blessed be God...)
3. We thank you for the tender love and care you give to us (Blessed be God...)
4. We ask for good health for ourselves and our children (Blessed be God...)
5. We ask for a safe and peaceful delivery (Blessed be God...)
6. We ask for the strength to accept and nurture this child (Blessed be God...)
7. We ask for the wisdom and courage to be the parents we are called to be (Blessed be God...)

8. We ask you to help us through the support of our family, our friends, and this faith community (Blessed be God...)

9. We ask you to instill in this child a deep and longing love for you, our God (Blessed be God...)

## BLESSING

Our community of faith now blesses you. As a sign of unity, please stand and extend your right hand in blessing over these parents. (The expectant parents are invited to place their hands on the mother's stomach.)

Holy are you, expectant parents, for you have been chosen by God for this purpose. The Holy Spirit has come upon you and you are full of grace. Our Lord is with you in a special way. Blessed are you among all peoples of today, and blessed is the fruit of your womb, the one chosen by God. Amen.

# ETHNIC RITUALS AND TRADITIONS

Along with food and affection, parents pass on to young children a vision of life. That vision helps children gain a sense of who they are as individuals and as family, and of what the world is like. It helps young people make sense of their lives and provides a foundation for all later learnings about life as a man or woman, how people should interact, and what values are worth living out. This vision of life is often referred to as "culture." Often, as parents struggle to articulate the vision of life they want to share with their children, they realize that many of the values they themselves hold were passed on through family and ethnic traditions. Behind simple family stories, ethnic customs, and national celebrations lies a vision of life. Reclaiming ethnic traditions as a family provides a way of claiming the values we live by and celebrating our connectedness with family members who came before. It provides a way of celebrating our values not just in words, but also in food and decor, song and dance.

As a catholic, or universal, community, the Roman Catholic Church holds people of many different national and ethnic groups in its embrace. Their presence provides the church community with great richness and an equally great responsibility. The richness is obvious—a tapestry of experiences and traditions that bears witness to God's continuing presence among people. The responsibility, sometimes less obvious, is twofold:

1. To be attentive to the ways in which God's love has been revealed through the culture and traditions of the local community;
2. To help the entire church community to view God and the Gospel call from a multicultural perspective, affirming and celebrating the many different ways in which God has been made known in our midst.

The implications of this responsibility for parishes are likewise dual.

First, parishes need to be conscious of the racial, national, and ethnic mix of the families in their faith community. The unique values, traditions, and prayer rituals of each group should be taken into account as parish celebrations are scheduled, planned, and celebrated. In some cultures there is a strong and consistent tradition of family and community prayer. Where such a tradition exists it should be supported. Where traditions have been lost, the parish can act to help people retrieve their heritage and reclaim their traditions.

Second, parishes need to help all families grow in their comfort with people of different cultures and traditions. As one of the few, truly multicultural groups in U.S. society, the Church can play a major role in helping increase their comfort with, and appreciation of, people of different racial, national and ethnic groups. Exposing parish members to the different ethnic groups that make up the one Catholic Church, incorporating traditions from other cultures in parish worship, and providing families with prayer resources that help them to better understand and pray with people of other cultural groups helps family members to claim their membership in a much wider family—the multi-cultured and multi-colored family of God.

## QUINCE AÑOS CELEBRATION [5]

The *Quince Años* celebration is just one example of a deep-rooted cultural tradition that deserves to be affirmed and celebrated by the contemporary Church. *Quince años* means 15 years in Spanish. This popular ceremony that marks the passage from childhood to adult life traces its roots to the native peoples of Latin America.

When Spanish missionaries arrived in Mexico in the 1500s, they found the Aztecs and the Maya practicing some rich religious traditions. Life for the natives was sacred; their whole lives revolved around their gods, temples, and religious events. In order to find favor with their gods, they ritualized every critical stage of life from birth to death. One such ceremony was the initiation rites at puberty, which consisted primarily of separating the child from his or her mother, introducing the child to the sacred, and initiating him or her into a life of service to the community. The elements of such ceremonies varied from group to group. The Maya ceremony was particularly interesting and very elaborate. Sylvanus G. Morley describes it in great detail in his book *The Ancient Maya* (Stanford University Press).

The Maya always designated a special day for the puberty rites, a day they believed to portend good fortune. A leader of the town was appointed to sponsor all the boys and girls participating in the rites. The sponsor's task was to assist the priest during the rites and to furnish the feast that followed. Four honorable old men called *chacs* assisted the sponsor and the priest.

On the day of the ceremony, all participants gathered in the courtyard of the sponsor's house which was purified by the priest to drive out evil spirits. Godparents were picked—an old man for the boys and an old woman for the girls.

---

[5] The Quince Años Celebration was contributed by Angela Erevia, MCDP.

The *chacs* then placed on the children's heads pieces of white cloth brought by the mothers. The older children were asked if they had committed any sin. If they said "yes," they were separated from the others. (We do not know whether they were excluded from further participation in the rites.) The priest ordered everyone to be seated and to preserve absolute silence. He then pronounced a benediction on the children.

Next the sponsor of the ceremony tapped each child nine times on the forehead with a bone given to him by the priest, moistening their foreheads, faces, and the spaces between their fingers and toes with water.

After this anointing, the priest removed the white cloths from the children's heads. The boys and girls then gave the *chacs* gifts of feathers and cacao beans. The priest cut the white beads which the boys wore on their heads. Pipe-smoking attendants gave the children a puff of smoke. The youth were then given food brought by their mothers, and a wine offering was made to the gods.

The mothers removed from their daughters the red shell each wore as a symbol of purity, indicating that they had reached the age for marriage. First the girls were dismissed, and then the boys. When the children had gone, the parents passed out presents to the officials and the spectators—pieces of cotton cloth. The ceremony then ended with much eating and drinking.

Clearly, these puberty rites situated young people within the adult life of their community, and they had a profoundly religious character: A priest conducted the ceremony. The elderly took the important role of godparents. The parents provided gifts which were integral to the ceremony. A confession and benediction signified the reconciliation of the young with the people of their community. The period of silence indicated serious reflection on what was happening. A feast was given in the young people's honor. The whole ceremony was designed to recognize and affirm the young people.

Today as in the days of the Maya, young people need the recognition and affirmation of adults as they search for their own personal identity. Adolescents, who are going through one of the most difficult periods of life, need significant people to surround them with love and care so that they may develop their self-esteem and believe in themselves.

One way that Hispanics do this is through the celebration of a young person's life at age 15, the age at which an intense push towards adulthood begins. A well-planned *quince años* enriches not only the 15-year-olds but their families and friends as well.

In preparation for the celebration—a Mass of Thanksgiving—the young people and all the persons involved take formal instruction. Lessons include a brief history of the *quince años* tradition and the reasons for celebrating it. Participants also explore the idea that God is calling the young people to be prophets of their times, to articulate new ways of living the Christian values of the Gospel. The value of peer-to-peer ministry is also stressed. A study of the Sacraments of Initiation is a key part of the program, focusing on new ways for the young people to celebrate their Christian commitment. Most of them were baptized as infants; therefore, a fresh look at baptism, Eucharist, and confirmation helps them to be more aware of their dignity and their place within the family and the Church community. Far in advance of the *quince años* celebration, there is a day of recollection that concludes with a celebration of the Sacrament of Reconciliation.

Finally, the day for *quince años* comes. The Mass begins with a procession at which time the youth may present the following gifts:

**Birth Certificate**: a symbol of gratitude to God and to their parents for the gift of life.

**Baptismal Robe**: a symbol of their putting on the mind and the heart of Christ.

**Baptismal Shoes**: a symbol of their walking in the footsteps of Christ and their willingness to walk with others so that they too may discover Christ in their lives and follow after Him.

**Baptismal Candle:** a symbol of Christ, the Light of the World, inviting them to be a light for one another and for us.

**Confirmation Recuerdo (Memento):** a symbol of the gifts of the Holy Spirit which made them holy people of God.

**Crown:** a symbol of their sharing in the mission of Christ as Priest, King, and Servant King.

The readings for a *quince años* Mass are carefully selected to emphasize the important role that the youth play in our family and in our Church community. At the appropriate times of the Mass, the young people are called by name. One such time is after the homily when they are called to stand before the Christian community to renew their baptismal promises. After Communion, they make an act of consecration to Our Lady of Guadalupe and offer a rose to Our Lady as a sign of their fidelity to Jesus, her Son. Before the concluding prayers, the parents give a special blessing to their son or daughter who is participating in the *quince años* celebration.

The Mass concluded, a fiesta follows with gifts for the youths. Essential to the fiesta are song, dancing, and food as family and friends gather to celebrate and thank God for the gift of their 15-year-old's life!

# FAMILY RITUALS THROUGH THE DAY

In the initial essay of Section Two, Thomas Boland notes that "the seeds of the sacred are sown for Christian families in the field of everyday experience." Throughout the day, family members share numerous experiences that have the potential for opening their hearts and minds to the constancy and closeness of God's love. Simple rituals like grace before meals, bedtime prayers, or a quick departure blessing before family members head off to school or work can be powerful reminders of God's loving presence. They also provide a springboard for family members' appreciation of the other ways and other contexts in which God works in the world. Parishes can support and enhance the family celebration of everyday rituals by:

1. Raising the awareness of the parish community to the importance of home rituals;
2. Gathering like-minded families to share and learn from one another about how they pray as families;
3. Providing samples or simple resources for daily or occasional family prayer;
4. Including the ordinary events of family life (work, school and play; experiences of confusion and wonder) in the general intercession for parish liturgies.

# CONCLUSION

We hope that these ideas for integrating a family perspective into parish celebrations have sparked your own creativity. Parishes have marvelous opportunities to partner with families in ritual celebrations, whether they are the rituals of the year, family milestone rituals, ethnic rituals and traditions, or the rituals of family life through the day. These opportunities are waiting to be discovered and celebrated. Whatever form or approach you take, the important thing is that your parish begins or strengthens its efforts with families.

# 2

# TABLE: POSSIBILITIES FOR
# FAMILY-PARISH RITUAL PARTNERSHIP

Using the ideas in this section and the resources in *Family Rituals and Celebrations*, here is a guide to the possibilities for forging a family-parish ritual partnership.

**FAMILY RITUAL** .................................................... **PARISH RITUAL**

## *FAMILIES CELEBRATING RITUALS THROUGH THE YEAR*

### Advent Season

Family Advent Wreath and Blessing ......................... Parish Advent Wreath and Blessing
Family Jesse Tree .......................................................... Parish Jesse Tree

### Christmas Season

Blessing for a Family Christmas Tree ...................... Blessing for the Parish Christmas Tree
Family Christmas Creche and Blessing .................. Parish Christmas Creche and Blessing

## FAMILIES CELEBRATING RITUAL MILESTONES

First Day of School and Last Day of School .......... Remembrance at Sunday Eucharist
Celebration of Birthdays ................... Regular Remembrance at Sunday Eucharist
Wedding Anniversary .................... Monthly Blessings of Married Couples
Graduation ................... Parish Eucharist for Graduates and Families
At Home Celebration When A Child Marries .......... Celebration of Sacrament of Marriage
Retirement ................... Yearly Parish Celebration of Retirement
Wake Service: Death in the Family ................ Parish Eucharist, Burial
Remembering the Death of a Loved One .......... Regular Remembrance at Sunday Eucharist

## FAMILIES CELEBRATING ETHNIC RITUALS AND TRADITIONS

The Home Altar ................... Parish Family Shrine or Chapel
Ethnic Traditions ................... Corresponding Parish Celebrations

## FAMILIES CELEBRATING RITUALS THROUGH THE DAY

Blessing for a Family or Household .......... Annual Blessing of Families or Households
Family Celebration of God's Forgiveness .......... Community Celebration of Reconciliation

# ACTIVITIES:
# DISCOVERING FAMILY RITUALS

## *FAITH MAURO, RSM*

"Activities: Discovering Family Rituals" will help parish staff assist families in discovering the religious significance of life experiences and events, and the possibilities for parish and family ritual celebrations. These activities are short and flexible so that they can be used in any number of settings or programs in a parish or combined into a family program or a parent workshop. They can also be used with a parish liturgical committee or groups preparing ritual celebrations with or for families.

## ACTIVITY #1: RECALLING CELEBRATIONS

### *FAMILY ACTIVITY[1]*

Distribute a sheet of paper to each participant or family. Guide the participants or families through the following steps:

a. Ask each family to think of two activities or celebrations that the family does together. Give them a few minutes to think. (These can be rituals of family life, ethnic traditions, rituals through the year, and/or ritual milestones. See the presentation below for further commentary.)

b. Compile a list of everyone's ideas and add any that the group wants to add that perhaps were not on individual lists.

---

[1] Contributed by Antoinette Purcell, OSB.

c. As a family share what you can about the rituals using the following questions as a guide:

- How did these rituals originate?
- Why are they significant either to individuals or to the family?
- Have they changed over the years? If so, what brought about the changes?
- How has God been present or how has God been discovered/celebrated in these rituals?
- How are the rituals connected to the "world" beyond the family? (Are any part of national, world, state, church tradition, etc.?)

## PRESENTATION ON FAMILY RITUALS

Rituals are essential for our family life. Family rituals give us a sense of permanence, the assurance that even the most ordinary of family activities are meaningful and significant. Many of those who study family life suggest that true meaning in daily living is only accomplished and maintained by family ritual, and that such concrete ways of acknowledging life's meaning are a prerequisite for the physical and emotional health of every family member. The family is able to develop its own sense of permanence and continuity by taking the time to fully attend to the simplest of family activities; by going beyond just "getting things done" to enjoying the sharing of doing things together; by acting with a sense of the honor conferred by the basic activities of family life, which are not chores or obligations, but opportunities to "be" together.

Ritual is born of celebration of family togetherness, through attention to and enjoyment of shared life activities which develop the family bond. Family ritual is making the effort to impart dignity and symbolism to the simple acts of eating together, going to bed, and rising in the morning. Family ritual is attempting to "share" rather than just "do" what life requires. Family ritual is not just saying grace at the dinner table; it is making the effort to help all of the family experience grace together, through the simple act of attending fully to being together for a meal. Whether it is ritualizing everyday patterns like getting up, eating together, or going to bed, or celebrating important milestones, like birthdays and graduations, the family needs to establish rituals which acknowledge life's meaning.

One of the ways that we encounter God is through the experiences and events of everyday life—in our work, in our relationships, and in our family life. We may not be accustomed to recognizing God's presence in the ordinary events of family life, but each of our family rituals has the potential of helping us discover God's presence. The rituals of everyday family life and of important milestones are opportunities to share faith in the family. It only takes a little planning and creativity to bring faith values into our daily life and special occasions. Our task as families is to identify and establish our own family rituals so that we may enrich our family relationships and discover God in our family life.

The Catholic tradition provides us with a variety of rituals which can impart a sense of permanence to the ways we share faith in the family. Rituals are one of the primary ways through which the Catholic faith is shared from one generation to another. The liturgical year provides us with numerous opportunities for family rituals, especially around Advent and Christmas, Lent and Easter. Civic celebrations, like Martin Luther King, Jr. Day and Earth Day, likewise provide us with opportunities to celebrate our faith in the family or with other families throughout the year.

Our ethnic traditions provide us with family rituals to celebrate and share the Catholic faith. Ethnic traditions provide us with a sense of permanence and identity. For some families this will mean affirming the importance of ethnic rituals which have been celebrated in the family for generations. For other families this will mean reclaiming ethnic rituals that have been lost and, perhaps, finding new ways to celebrate these rituals. Our ethnic family rituals have the power to help us discover and celebrate God's presence.

Through the rituals of family life, the rituals of the Catholic tradition, and the rituals of ethnic traditions, faith can be nourished and celebrated in our families.

(See *Family Rituals and Celebrations* for actual rituals).

### FAMILY RITUALS SCRAPBOOK[2]

You might want to suggest that families make a book of rituals using drawings, snapshots, explanations, poems, reflections. Individual family members can add to the book by sharing their feelings about the event or simply recording the who, what, where, why, when of the event. This is a great way to pass on rituals to the next generation. It is also fun to see and read about them as time turns them into memories. Events of the "world" beyond the family could also be recorded in relation to the family ritual. In retrospect it could be revealing to see connections between family and world events.

# ACTIVITY #2: CELEBRATING LIFE EVENTS

### FAMILY CALENDAR ACTIVITY

Pass out copies of a one-month calendar. While quiet music plays, invite families to do the following:

1. Using the calendar, ask the families to make a list of the rituals of family life, ritual milestones, rituals of the Catholic tradition, and rituals of ethnic traditions which took place in their life in the last month. (You may need to review the presentation in Activity #1 for descriptions of each type of ritual.)

2. After they have completed the calendar, ask them what they discovered about their monthly pattern of family rituals. Surprises? Disappointments? etc.

---

[2] Contributed by Antoinette Purcell, OSB.

## PRESENTATION ON CELEBRATING
## FAMILY LIFE EVENTS

### OVERVIEW

●   Celebration is a time of coming together for affirming and remembering a significant moment. A celebration can be as simple as two friends, a glass of wine, a toast to good news. Celebrations may focus on events like birthdays, anniversaries, graduations, weddings, or on particular holidays like Christmas, Easter, First Eucharist, etc.

●   Ritual is a patterned way of doing something that includes symbol, movement and words, and is rooted in a common history. A ritual may be as simple as a good night kiss or a blessing, or as formal as the rituals which commonly take place on Thanksgiving, Christmas, or at the Easter Vigil.

●   There are three components of rituals:

    a. Symbols: gifts, food, and drink
    b. Words: singing, vows, toasts, blessings, storytelling, giving thanks
    c. Movement (gesture): dance, hugs, blessing signs

●   Rituals are natural to the human species. They are found in history and cultures everywhere. Common examples of rituals include birth rites and puberty rites.

●   Why do we ritualize?

    a. To explain the truths by which we live and the relationships which underlie our lives.
    b. To raise awareness of the meaning of everyday experiences.
    c. To affirm the goodness of creation and everyday life, to discover God in our everyday life experiences. This is the message of the incarnation of God in Jesus Christ. Any interaction in life has the *potential* of becoming religiously significant.
    d. To slow down the inner pace of our lives, to go deeper, and to seek meaning in our lives.

e. To demonstrate our connectedness; to be a part of something larger than ourselves; for support and a sense of belonging.

● Religious rituals seek to celebrate all of these purposes and help us to become aware of our relationship with God.

● Ritual is particularly important at times of transition, moments of crisis, developmental steps, and at times when we are vulnerable.

● The cycles of the day, month, season, and year can be ritualized.

● Some of the elements of ritual and celebration include: story-telling; symbol-making; blessing; sharing food, drink and conversation; gift-giving; singing; dancing; envisioning; making commitments; affirming; giving thanks.

## EXAMPLES OF THE POTENTIAL OF FAMILY RITUALS:

| forgiveness | being able to say "I'm sorry" |
|---|---|
| tolerance | respecting cultural differences |
| kindness | helping a friend |
| gratitude | saying "thank you" |
| hospitality | welcoming playmates, friends |
| gentleness | witnessing parent-to-parent interactions |
| patience | parents listening to teens |
| understanding | healing a heartbreak disappointment |
| sharing | sharing popcorn, hair dryer, TV, etc |

## CATEGORIES OF ORDINARY LIFE EXPERIENCES
## TO RITUALIZE AND CELEBRATE:

- Welcoming New Members: arrival of a new baby; remarriage; adoption; a new pet; new animals
- Leave Taking: death; divorce; going to college; leaving home; loss of friends
- Reconciling: handling disagreements; resolving conflict
- Welcoming Home: coming home from hospital or nursing home; daily return from work or school; family member who has been away
- Sending Forth: to camp, basketball game; volunteering; new job; new school; job experience
- Playing: putting to bed; vacation; TV; leisure; games
- Times of Crises: injury; sickness; loss; disappointments; unemployments; loss of the family farm
- Firsts: driving the tractor; driver's license; date; loss of tooth; start school; move away from home
- Seasons: planting; harvesting; vacation; opening of school; quinceañera
- Serving: doing chores; visiting the ill; taking food to a neighbor; visiting a funeral home; harvesting; helping a sick neighbor; writing a letter
- Accomplishments: grades; new job; sports; musical; culinary; ribbons at the fair
- Caring/Nurturing: nursing; child-rearing; needs of elderly
- Failures: loss of job; not getting on a sports team

## A PROCESS FOR CELEBRATING FAMILY LIFE EVENTS

This process will help families turn "ordinary" family life experiences into ritual celebrations that have the potential of becoming religiously significant for them. You may wish to put the process on newsprint so that the participants have a visual aid to see how to enhance and celebrate an event.

1. Ask the participants to name an event in their family's life that they would like to ritualize or celebrate. Ask

them to refer back to their one month calendar. They can also select a milestone like graduating from high school.

2. Which category of celebration does your experience fit (e.g., leave taking; sending forth; accomplishments, etc.)?

3. What are some of the elements of celebration that can be brought to this experience (e.g., story-telling; gift-giving; affirming; etc.)?

4. How might your family incorporate these elements into a family celebration or ritual? (Example: for a graduation invite guests to bring pictures of times they have shared with graduate and create a memory album.)

# ACTIVITY #3: CELEBRATING RITES OF PASSAGE

## FAMILY RITES OF PASSAGE ACTIVITY

Distribute a sheet of paper to each participant or family. Guide the participants or families through the following steps. Quiet, instrumental music can be played during this time.

1. Which major rite of passage has most recently been experienced by your family (e.g., birth; coming to maturity; chosen life style commitments; death.) Describe the event briefly. (See the presentation for explanations of each major rite of passage.)

2. What were the "stages" of this event?

3. What family rituals were associated with these stages?

4. What parish rituals were associated with these stages?

5. How could the parish church help ritualize the stages of this major rite of passage?

## PRESENTATION ON RITES OF PASSAGE

● Identify the major life passages: birth; coming to maturity; chosen life style commitments; death. Discuss some of the dynamics that are involved with each of these passages and how they affect families. Connect these major rites of passage to the Church's sacramental system.

Here is an example of the dynamics for chosen life commitments, which involve four stages: call, preparation, commitment, and lifestyle.

|  | Marriage | Priesthood/ Religious Life | Single |
|---|---|---|---|
| Call | Courtship | Discernment | Discernment |
| Preparation | Engagement | Seminary/ Novitiate | Life Experiences |
| Commitment | Wedding Vows | Ordination/ Vows | Live beyond self |
| Lifestyle | Life together | Celibate/ Community Life | Alone/ Community |

● Look at family rituals. Take a rite of passage and the events that surround it, e.g., birth. Explore ways we can help families celebrate these events.

● Explore ways that each life passage can be enhanced and celebrated in the family and the parish. Involve the participants in this process. You may want to put this information on newsprint.

**RESOURCE:** "A Family View of Rites of Passage." Edwin Friedman. *Growing in Faith: A Catholic Family Sourcebook*, ed. John Roberto (New Rochelle: Don Bosco Multimedia, 1990).

## *PLANNING TOGETHER*

Give each family a piece of newsprint and a marker. Ask them to take a rite of passage (perhaps the one they identified in Step One), and ask them to develop ideas for strengthening the celebration of the rite of passage.

- What will we, as families, do at home to celebrate these rites of passage more fully?
- What can the parish community do to celebrate these rites more fully?

# Section Six

# RESOURCES

# RESOURCES ON FAMILY AND RITUAL

The following resources have been selected because they either focus on family and ritual or provide insights and/or resources applicable to family and parish ritual.

## FOUNDATIONAL UNDERSTANDINGS

Apostolos-Cappadona, Diane, editor. *The Sacred Play of Children*. San Francisco: Harper and Row, 1983.

Berstein, CSJ, Eleanor. *Liturgy and Spirituality in Context*. Collegeville, MN: Liturgical Press, 1990.

Boff, Leonardo. *Sacraments of Life, Life of the Sacraments*. Washington, DC: Pastoral Press, 1987.

Bowman, FSPA, Thea, editor. *Families Black and Catholic; Catholic and Black*. Washington, DC: United States Catholic Conference, 1985.

Boyer, Ernest. *Finding God at Home—Family Life as Spiritual Discipline*. San Francisco: Harper and Row, 1984.

Browning Robert L. and Roy A. Reed. *The Sacraments in Religious Education and Liturgy*. Birmingham: Religious Education Press, 1985.

Collins OSB, Mary. *Worship: Renewal to Practice*. Washington, DC: Pastoral Press, 1987.

Fischer, Kathleen. *The Inner Rainbow: The Imagination in Christian Life*. New York: Paulist Press, 1983.

Fleming, Austin. *Preparing for Liturgy—A Theology and Spirituality*. Washington, DC: Pastoral Press, 1985.

Francis, CSV, Mark R. *Liturgy in a Multicultural Community*. Collegeville, MN: Liturgical Press, 1991.

National Conference of Catholic Bishops. *Plenty Good Room—The Spirit and Truth of African American Catholic Worship.* Washington, DC: United States Catholic Conference, 1991.

Nelson, Gertrud Mueller. *To Dance with God—Family Ritual and Community Celebration.* New York: Paulist Press, 1986.

Ostdiek, Gilbert. *Catechesis for Liturgy—A Program for Parish Involvement.* Washington, DC: Pastoral Press, 1986.

Perez, Arturo. *Popular Catholicism—A Hispanic Perspective.* Washington, DC: The Pastoral Press, 1988.

Roberto, John, editor. *Access Guide to Youth Ministry: Liturgy and Worship.* New Rochelle: Don Bosco Multimedia, 1990.

Romero, Gilbert C. *Hispanic Devotional Piety—Tracing the Biblical Roots.* Maryknoll: Orbis Books, 1991.

Westerhoff III, John H. *Learning Through Liturgy.* New York: Seabury Press, 1978.

————— and William Willimon. *Liturgy and Learning Through the Life Cycle.* New York: Seabury Press, 1980.

Wilde, James, editor. *At That Time—Cycles and Seasons in the Life of Christians.* Chicago: Liturgy Training Publications, 1989.

Wright, Wendy M. *Sacred Dwelling—A Spirituality of Family Life.* New York: Crossroad, 1990.

## LITURGY & WORSHIP RESOURCES

Bailey, Betty Jane and J. Martin. *Youth Plan Worship.* New York: Pilgrim Press, 1987.

Benson, Dennis. *Creative Worship in Youth Ministry.* Loveland, CO: Group Books, 1985.

Cassa, Yvonne and Joanne Sanders. *Groundwork—Planning Liturgical Seasons.* Chicago: Liturgy Training Publications, 1982.

Cawkwell, David, et al. *At Home with the Word.* (Annual) Chicago: Liturgy Training Publications, 1992.

Hilliard, Dick and Beverly Valenti-Hilliard. *Come & Celebrate: More Center Celebrations.* Notre Dame, IN: Ave Maria Press, 1985.

Hock, Mary Isabelle. *Worship through the Seasons.* San Jose: Resource Publications, 1987.

Huck, Gabe, editor. *Liturgy with Style and Grace: A Basic Manual for Planners and Ministers.* Revised Edition. Chicago: Liturgy Training Publications, 1984.

Huck, Gabe et al. *Hymnal for Catholic Students: Leader's Manual.* Chicago: GIA Publications and Liturgy Training Publications, 1989. (Includes the *Directory of Masses with Children*, background essays, and 20 celebrations.)

Johnson, Lawrence. *The Word and Eucharist Handbook.* San Jose: Resource Publications, 1986.

Krier, Catherine H. *Symbols for All Seasons—Environmental Planning for Cycles A, B, & C.* San Jose: Resource Publications, 1988.

Marchal, Michael. *Adapting the Liturgy—Creative Ideas for the Church Year.* San Jose: Resource Publications, 1989.

Miffleton, Jack. *Sunday's Child—A Planning Guide for Liturgies with both Children and Adults.* (1989).

Nelson, Gertrud Mueller. *To Dance with God—Family Ritual and Community Celebration.* New York: Paulist Press, 1986.

Reeves SC, Sister John Maria and Sister Maureen Roe RSM. *Junior High Liturgy, Prayer, Reconciliation.* Villa Maria, PA: Center for Learning, 1988.

Ryan, G. Thomas, et al. *Sourcebook for Sundays and Seasons—An Almanac of Parish Liturgy.* (Annual) Chicago: Liturgy Training Publications, 1992.

Walden, Carol, editor. *Called to Create—Christian Witness and the Arts.* San Jose: Resource Publications, 1986.

## PRAYER & RITUAL RESOURCES

Alternatives. *To Celebrate—Reshaping Holidays & Rites of Passage.* Ellenwood, GA: Alternatives, 1987.

Black, Barbara, Karen Jessie and John Paulett. *Pentecost, Peanuts, Popcorn, Prayer—Prayer Services for High School Students.* Villa Maria, PA: Center for Learning, 1988.

Center for Learning. *Seasonal Liturgies.* Villa Maria, PA: Center for Learning, 1989.

Costello, Gwen. *Praying with Children—28 Prayer Services for Various Occasions*. Mystic, CT: Twenty-Third Publications, 1990.

Cronin, Gaynell Bordes. *Holy Days and Holidays—Prayer Celebrations with Children (Volume II)*. San Francisco: Harper and Row, 1988.

————. *Holy Days and Holidays—Prayer Celebrations with Children (Volume I)*. Revised Edition. Hagerstown, MD: Winston Press, 1985.

Curran, Dolores. *Family Prayer*. Mystic, CT: Twenty-Third Publications, 1983.

DeGidio, Sandra. *Enriching Faith through Family Celebrations*. Mystic, CT: Twenty-Third Publications, 1989.

Diller, Harriet. *Celebrations that Matter—A Year-round Guide to Making Holidays Meaningful*. Minneapolis: Augsburg, 1990.

Donze, ASC, Mary Terese. *Prayer and Our Children—Passing on the Tradition*. Notre Dame, IN: Ave Maria Press, 1987.

Duck, Ruth C. and Maren C. Tirabassi. *Touch Holiness—Resources for Worship*. New York: Pilgrim Press, 1990.

Dues, Greg. *Seasonal Prayer Services for Teenagers*. Mystic, CT: Twenty-Third Publications, 1990.

Hays, Edward. *Prayers for the Domestic Church—A Handbook for Worship in the Home*. Easton, KS: Forest of Peace Books, 1979.

Hesch, John B. *Prayer and Meditation for Middle School Kids*. New York: Paulist Press, 1985.

Jeep, Elizabeth McMahon. *Children's Daily Prayer—For the School Year*. (Annual) Chicago: Liturgy Training Publications, 1992.

*Junior High Liturgy, Prayer, Reconciliation*. Villa Maria, PA: Center for Learning, 1987.

Kelley, Gail. *Traditionally Yours—Telling the Christian Story through Family Traditions*. San Jose: Resource Publications, 1987.

Lieberman, Susan Abel. *New Traditions—Redefining Celebrations for Today's Family*. New York: Noonday Press, 1991.

Link, Mark. *Challenge*. Allen, TX: Tabor, 1988.

Manternach, Janann, with Carl Pfeifer. *And the Children Pray*. Notre Dame, IN: Ave Maria Press, 1989.

Mathson, Patricia. *Pray and Play—28 Prayers Services and Activities for Children in K through Sixth Grade.* Notre Dame, IN: Ave Maria Press, 1989.

McDonnell, Rea. *Prayer Pilgrimage through Scripture.* New York: Paulist Press. 1984.

Nelson, Gertrud Mueller. *To Dance with God—Family Ritual and Community Celebration.* New York: Paulist Press, 1986.

*Prayer Forms.* Mystic, CT: Twenty-Third Publications, 1987.

*Prayer Service Models.* Villa Maria, PA: Center for Learning, 1984.

Sanders, Corinne, and Judith Bisignano. *Seasonal Celebrations.* Kansas City: Sheed and Ward, 1985.

Schaffran, Janet. *More than Words.* Oak Park, IL: Meyer Stone Books, 1988.

Sears, Marge. *Life Cycle Celebrations for Women.* Mystic, CT: Twenty-Third Publications, 1989.

Weiderkehr, Macrina. *Seasons of Your Heart—Prayers and Reflections.* (Revised Edition) San Francisco: Harper, 1991.

Winter, Miriam Therese. *Woman Prayer, Woman Song.* Oak Park, IL: Meyer Stone Books, 1987.

## VIDEOS TO HELP FAMILIES PRAY AND CELEBRATE RITUALS

Here are several videos you can use with families to prepare for family prayer or for family rituals. Consult *Media, Faith, and Families: A Parents' Guide to Family Viewing* and *Media, Faith, and Families: A Parish Ministry Guide* for additional video suggestions for sharing faith in the family.

**Advent: A Time to Hope.** Kathleen Chesto uses simple family events to teach about our Catholic faith. Advent is a season of waiting. The experience of parents/family awaiting the birth of their child speaks volumes about waiting in hope for God to break through and transform our everyday lives. [20 minutes, Twenty-Third Publications]

**Celebrating the Church Year for Children.** A series of innovative video programs which attempt to convey the power and beauty of Church seasons and events. [15 minutes each—6 segments, Paulist Press]
**Titles:** *Advent, Christmas, Days of Mary, Lent, Easter, Pentecost*

**Helping Children (and everyone else) Pray.** Adults hunger for a deeper personal prayer life and are eager to introduce children to the practice of prayer. Sister Marlene Halpin provides a solid background for catechists, parents, and other parish ministers to help themselves and others integrate prayer into their lives. [20 minutes each part—1 video, Tabor Publishing]
**Titles:** *Exploring Your Own Prayer Life, Praying Together, Planning New Ways to Pray Together.*

**Journey to Easter.** Enjoy this seven-part program, one segment for each week of Lent and Easter, as a resource for the home or parish. The viewer is guided on a journey to Easter through the use of Scripture, drama, and stories that deal with the concerns of life and the joys of our reunions with Christ. [15 minutes each—7 segments Oblate Media and Franciscan Communications]

**Little Visits With God.** Families for generations have made the best-selling book "More Little Visits with God" a vital part of their sharing times. Now bring children the same faith-building opportunities along with the excitement and impact of video. [70 minutes each—2 videos, Don Bosco Multimedia]
**Volume 1:** A video of family devotions; each story is five to eight minutes, either animated, live, or puppet. The guide includes discussion questions, Scripture reading, and prayer for each story.
**Volume 2:** Ten additional stories include the power of prayer, forgiveness, watching your words, and more...

**Loaves of Thanksgiving.** Many parishioners perceive the Mass as a routine and repetitious ceremony rather than a celebration. *Loaves of Thanksgiving* presents the five aspects of the liturgy that call us to a greater understanding of what celebrating the Eucharist really means. Through real life minidramas, the video reveals ways in which participating in the Eucharist transforms peoples' lives and so begins to transform parish life. We come to see that faith, participation, worship, community, and sacrifice are all symbolic "loaves" of thanksgiving. [30 minutes, Franciscan Communications]

**Prayer in Your Home.** Modern life tends to disrupt families. Pressures of work, social commitments, hobbies, and leisure activities pull family members in different directions. *Prayer in Your Home* presents the enriching possibilities of family prayer under five symbolic home activities: sharing a meal, preparing for sleep, sharing our stories, experiencing consolation, and celebrating a special event. [30 minutes, Franciscan Communications]

**Preparing for Christmas I and II.** These are two four-part videos hosted by Fr. Anthony Scannell which use stories, songs, Scripture readings, dramatized stories, photography and reflective prayer. [11–18 minute segments—2 videos, Franciscan Communications]
**Part I:** *Waiting, Hoping, Preparing, Giving and Receiving.*
**Part II:** *The Child in Us, Santa Clausing, The Perfect Gift, The Journey to Bethlehem*

**The Seven Circles of Prayer.** Here is an inspiring combination of photography, dramatic vignettes, and commentary...all to help the viewer meet God in prayer. The image of seven concentric circles conveys a sense of wholeness to the life of prayer. Prayer is shown to be a very personal interior experience and yet as no escape from the world. [32 minutes, Oblate Media and Franciscan Communications]

**The Story Tree/Holidays.** A treasure to celebrate life! Elaine Ward presents charming tales of fun and fantasy that help children appreciate the religious meaning of various holidays. [4–10 minutes each—6 segments, Tabor Publishing]
**Titles:** *Colors, Spinner's Christmas Gift, On Halloween, A Beautiful Valentine, The Thanksgiving Feast, An Easter Story*

**The Story Tree/Manners and Caring**
Children enjoy the rich reward of caring for others. These delightful stories by Elaine Ward invite youngsters to live as children of God, to care for one another as God cares for them. [5–9 minutes each—6 segments, Tabor Publishing]
**Titles:** *Derrik the Dragon, Lunch with Arnie, D.D. the Donkey, I'm Sorry, Grandmother Bear's Story, The Riddle of the Jungle*